The Harcourt Guide

to

MLA Documentation

The Harcourt Guide

to

MLA Documentation

Linda Smoak Schwartz
Coastal Carolina University

Australia Canada Mexico Singapore Spain United Kingdom United States

The Harcourt Guide to MLA Documentation
Linda Smoak Schwartz

Publisher: *Earl McPeek*
Acquisitions Editor: *Julie McBurney*
Market Strategist: *John Meyers*
Project Editor: *Jon Davies*
Art Director: *Susan Journey*
Production Manager: *Cindy Young*

Printed in the United States of America
6 7 8 9 10 11 12   08 07 06 05 04 03

For more information contact Heinle, 25 Thomson Place, Boston, MA 02210 USA,
or you can visit our Internet site at http://www.heinle.com

For permission to use material from this text or product contact us:
Tel   1-800-730-2214
Fax   1-800-730-2215
Web   www.thomsonrights.com

ISBN: 0-15-506415-0

Library of Congress Catalog Card Number: 00-102537

To Albert Larry Schwartz; Robert Tracy Schwartz; Joe and Alice Smoak; Bob and Sylvia Schwartz; Catherine and Jim Eick; Rick and Rita Smoak; Julia, Paul, Jeanette, and Natalie Tucker; Barbara, Michael, Joshua, and Rachel Cheatham; and Leona and Nicholas Yonge for their unfailing support and understanding, and to my students at Coastal Carolina University, whose questions inspired the writing of this book.

[I]f I'd a knowed what a trouble it was to make a book I wouldn't a tackled it [. . .].

—Mark Twain, <u>The Adventures of Huckleberry Finn</u>

May the Schwartz be with you.

—Mel Brooks et al., <u>Space Balls</u>

PREFACE

The Harcourt Guide to MLA Documentation grew out of my desire to create a guide to MLA documentation that would be brief enough to be used as a supplement to a handbook or literature anthology, yet comprehensive enough to address all the documentation issues students might encounter in writing both general topic and literary analysis research papers. I wanted an MLA guide that would be suitable for the beginning student with virtually no experience using MLA-style documentation, yet sophisticated enough to be kept and used throughout the student's years in college. I wanted a guide that would help students find sources in a university library and on the Internet. And I wanted a guide that would help students evaluate the research materials they found, make more sophisticated choices about what information to include in their papers, and successfully integrate the best information they could find into their papers.

The Harcourt Guide covers the entire process of creating a research paper, including selecting and narrowing a topic; creating both a working outline and a working bibliography; finding and evaluating research materials in a library and online; taking notes; and writing, documenting, formatting, and revising a paper. It provides model citations for virtually any type of source a writer might need to include in the works-cited list of a documented paper.

Concise and easy to use, The Harcourt Guide is ideally suited to freshman researchers who could purchase this text as a supplement to the handbook or literature anthology in a first- or second-semester composition course and retain it for use as a reference throughout their college careers. This text is also suitable for any sophomore-, junior-, or senior-level course in which papers using MLA-style documentation are written. It is comprehensive enough to function as the primary text in classes devoted entirely to research and has been successfully classroom tested in research seminars.

Notable features of The Harcourt Guide to MLA Documentation:

- Explains how to find sources in a library as well as on the Internet (chapter 3)
- Includes an annotated list of print, library subscription, and free online reference databases (chapter 3)
- Explains how to evaluate both print and Internet sources (chapter 3)
- Covers word-processing strategies such as how to create a hanging indent (chapter 8)

- Features fully annotated literary analysis and general topic sample research papers (chapters 6–7) and explains how to write literary analysis papers as well as general topic papers

- Explains how to quote from novels, short stories, plays, and poems, as well as from the critics who analyze them (chapter 16)

- Takes illustrative materials from classic literary works with which most readers should be familiar or from critical analyses of familiar works

- Features three sample outlines (chapters 4, 6, and 7)

- Features four sample bibliographies—one of which is cross-referenced —and a sample entry from an annotated bibliography (chapters 6–8)

- Gives a user-friendly checklist of exactly what information needs to be included in the citation after each model citation (chapters 9–13)

- Devotes a complete chapter to documenting various types of articles taken from scholarly journals, popular magazines, and newspapers (chapter 10)

- Clarifies many issues that often confuse beginning writers, such as the difference between continuously and noncontinuously paginated scholarly journals (chapter 10)

- Features model citations for many sources beginning writers have trouble documenting, such as telephone and personal interviews, letters, posters, maps, cartoons, advertisements, movies, television shows, radio shows, LP liner notes, compact disc booklets, and materials taken from literary anthologies and critical editions of literary works (chapters 9 and 11)

- Devotes an entire chapter to documenting materials taken from a wide variety of Internet sources (chapter 12)

- Gives model citations for materials taken from print, microform, CD-ROM, library subscription, and free online encyclopedias, dictionaries, and reference databases (chapter 13)

- Explains the use of square brackets to change the case of letters, clarify pronouns, change verb tenses, give further explanation, and indicate errors in a source (chapter 17) and illustrates these strategies in the sample papers (chapters 6–7)

- Devotes an entire chapter to the use of the bracketed ellipsis—one of the most recent changes in MLA documentation style (chapter 18)— and illustrates the use of the bracketed ellipsis in both sample papers (chapters 6–7)

My goal in writing <u>The Harcourt Guide</u> was to make writing a research paper using MLA-style documentation as simple and as easy as possible. I hope you will enjoy using this text and look forward to hearing your suggestions for future editions.

Linda Smoak Schwartz

ACKNOWLEDGMENTS

This book summarizes, explains, and interprets the guidelines created by the Modern Language Association of America for documenting research papers. It is designed to guide undergraduate writers of both general topic and literary analysis research papers. This work is not an official publication of the MLA, however, and has not been endorsed by that organization. If you have any questions about the MLA documentation style not addressed in this book, you should consult the two official publications of the Modern Language Association of America:

Gibaldi, Joseph. <u>MLA Handbook for Writers of Research Papers</u>. 5th ed. New York: MLA, 1999.

Gibaldi, Joseph. <u>MLA Style Manual and Guide to Scholarly Publishing</u>. 2nd ed. New York: MLA, 1998.

I am grateful to my colleagues in the English, theater, business, and education departments and in the Honors Program at Coastal Carolina University who classroom-tested this text and encouraged me enormously in the writing process: Maria K. Bachman, John P. Beard, Lee Bollinger, Donald O. Brook, Daniel J. Ennis, Jacqueline L. Gmuca, Steven L. Hamelman, Linda P. Hollandsworth, Rebecca L. (Tommye) Imschweiler, Linda Cooper Knight, Peter C. Lecouras, David E. Millard, Donald J. Millus, R. Ray Moye, Steven J. Nagle, Sarah J. (Sally) Purcell, Nelljean M. Rice, S. Paul Rice, Penelope S. (Penny) Rosner, Karlene G. Rudolph, Sara L. Sanders, Clifford A. Saunders, Jill L. Sessoms, Sara J. Sabota, Glenda Y. Sweet, Suzanne W. Thompson, Jennifer J. Viereck, Randall A. Wells, and W. Horace Wood.

In addition, I am grateful to Margaret H. (Peggy) Bates, Micheline B. Brown, Sallie D. Clarkson, Margaret A. Fain, Allison Faix, Michael M. Lackey, Matthew S. Haggard (reference assistant), Jeri L. Traw, and all of Coastal Carolina's wonderful librarians for technical assistance and moral support; to William E. Files, Caitlin Crawford-Lamb, and Jessica Lynn Piezzo for granting me permission to use their research papers or parts thereof; to Micheline B. Brown for her much appreciated help with the index; to Karen Moore and Julie McBurney at Harcourt College Publishers for believing in this project, and to Jon Davies, Melissa Gruzs, Kassandra Radomski, and the production staff at Harcourt for their excellent work on this text.

I am especially grateful to my colleagues at universities around the country who read this manuscript and offered their generous suggestions and encouragement at various stages of the revision process: John P. Beard, Coastal

Carolina University; Scott Douglass, Chattanooga State Technical Community College; Louie Edmundson, Chattanooga State Technical Community College; Steven L. Hamelman, Coastal Carolina University; Anne Maxham, Washington State University; Valerie A. Reimers, Southwestern Oklahoma State University; Helen J. Schwartz, Indiana University-Purdue University Indianapolis; Jill L. Sessoms, Coastal Carolina University; and Judith Williamson, Sauk Valley Community College.

About the Author

Linda Smoak Schwartz teaches courses in American and British literature and composition in the English Department at Coastal Carolina University, where she was Director of the Freshman Composition Program from 1982 until 1996. In addition, she directed Coastal's Sophomore Literature Program from 1992 until 1996. Her text <u>The Schwartz Guide to MLA Documentation</u> was published by McGraw-Hill in 1998. She lives in Conway, South Carolina, a small southern town a few miles inland from South Carolina's beautiful Grand Strand.

CONTENTS

The Harcourt Guide

to

MLA Documentation

CHAPTER 1

Why Do I Have to Write a Research Paper?

It's an unbelievably beautiful Monday, and having enjoyed a restful weekend just hanging out with your friends, you feel unusually energetic and happy when you wake up. You leave home and head to your first class of the day. Professor Smith enters the room smiling, and as the class begins, he announces the due date for the semester research paper and begins recommending topics you might want to consider.

You feel the energy and joy suddenly draining out of your body to be replaced with fear and dread. Four weeks to write the paper that may well determine whether you get the A you're determined to earn in this course. There's so much work you already have to do: midterm exams in almost every class, that trip to your best friend's wedding next week, that big party out at the lake on the 29th, papers due in several other classes. How will you ever get everything done? "Why do I have to write a research paper?" you ask yourself.

Your professors will ask you to write research papers because they want to train you to become an independent scholar who can locate information in any library and on the Internet, assess the value and reliability of that information, combine what you have learned with your own original ideas, and present your conclusions in a clear and understandable style. Your professors know that the ability to successfully research any topic you need to know about will serve you well not only during your college years but in whatever career you choose.

When you graduate from college and are hired for your first job, it is likely that you will not know everything there is to know about the company you work for, the products it manufactures, or the services it provides. Hopefully, you will have learned some strategies and skills during your college years that will be invaluable in whatever job you choose. However, it is likely that the company hiring you will give you some on-the-job training which will turn you into the knowledgeable, indispensable employee they hope you will become.

In this highly technological modern world, what is true in January may have been disproved by March, so it will always be necessary for you to keep up with the latest developments in your field. You won't have your professors around to keep you informed about all these changes, so in the professional world you will have to become the independent scholar your professors were training you to become. Never forget that information is power. If you know a great deal about a subject, you become a valuable resource person to

1

others who wish to learn about that subject. You become the employee most likely to get those promotions and raises.

Always remember, however, that the goal of research is not just to find out what others have written about a subject. Anyone can do that. The ultimate goal of research is to analyze a subject and present your own original analysis of it. The originality of thought you bring to your discussion of a topic you've researched is the magic ingredient that makes your paper or report worth reading or your presentation worth listening to.

CHAPTER 2

Using MLA and Other Styles of Documentation

Because you will undoubtedly be required to write numerous research papers if you plan to earn a degree from any college or university, you should be aware that there are numerous documentation styles you may be asked to use depending on the subject for which you are writing a particular paper.

Modern Language Association (MLA) Style

Papers written for courses in the humanities (English, history, philosophy, religion, art, music, theater) are usually documented in the style recommended by the Modern Language Association of America (MLA).

This book summarizes the guidelines created by the Modern Language Association of America for writing and documenting general topic and literary analysis research papers. If you have any questions about the MLA documentation style not addressed in this book, you should consult the two official publications of the Modern Language Association of America:

Gibaldi, Joseph. MLA Handbook for Writers of Research Papers.

   5th ed. New York: MLA, 1999.

Gibaldi, Joseph. MLA Style Manual and Guide to Scholarly Pub-

   lishing. 2nd ed. New York: MLA, 1998.

The MLA Handbook is designed for the use of undergraduate writers of research papers, and the MLA Style Manual is designed to guide graduate students writing theses and dissertations and professors writing articles and books for publication. Look for them in your university library if you need more information than this guide includes.

The Modern Language Association also maintains a Web site through which you can order MLA publications and find information about the most recent updates of the MLA documentation guidelines: <http://www.mla.org>.

American Psychological Association (APA) Style

Professors in education, psychology, and sociology usually require you to use APA style documentation: <http://www.apa.org>.

American Psychological Association. <u>Publication Manual of the</u>

<u>American Psychological Association</u>. 4th ed. Washington:

American Psychological Association, 1994.

Chicago Manual of Style (Chicago/CMS) Style

If you are preparing a manuscript for publication, you may need to use Chicago style documentation, which uses the footnote/endnote method of documenting sources. History professors sometimes require this style of documentation. Web information is available at <http://www.cms.org>.

<u>The Chicago Manual of Style</u>. 14th ed. Chicago: U of Chicago

P, 1993.

American Political Science Association (APSA) Style

Political science professors may ask you to follow the guidelines published by the American Political Science Association: <http://www.apsanet.org>.

Lane, Michael K. <u>Style Manual for Political Science</u>. Rev. ed.

Washington: American Political Science Association, 1993.

Linguistic Society of America (LSA) Style

Linguistics professors may require you to submit papers documented according to the guidelines published by the Linguistic Society of America in the <u>LSA Bulletin</u> every December. These guidelines may also be found on the LSA Web site: <http://www.lsadc.org>.

Council of Biology Editors (CBE) Style

Biology professors typically require you to use CBE style documentation: <http://www.cbe.org>.

Huth, Edward J. <u>Scientific Style and Format: The CBE Manual for</u>

<u>Authors, Editors, and Publishers</u>. 6th ed. Bethesda, MD:

Council of Biology Editors, 1994.

American Chemical Society (ACS) Style

Chemistry professors may require you to use ACS style documentation: <http://pubs.acs.org>.

Dodd, Janet S. The ACS Style Guide: A Manual for Authors and

    Editors. 2nd ed. Washington: American Chemical Society,

    1997.

American Mathematical Society (AMS) Style

For papers in mathematics, follow the documentation guidelines of the American Mathematical Society: <http://www.ams.org>.

O'Sean, Arlene, and Antoinette Schleyer. Mathematics into Type.

    Rev. ed. Providence, RI: American Mathematical Society,

    1999.

CHAPTER 3

Choosing a Topic and Finding Sources

Choosing an Appropriate Research Strategy

There is no one right way to research a subject. This text suggests some strategies you will hopefully find useful as you discover through the experience of actually gathering and evaluating information and writing papers what research strategies work best for you.

Consider creating a list of the tasks you must complete in the process of preparing the paper. Estimate how much time you will need

- to zero in on an interesting topic or
- to figure out what aspect of a subject you will research;
- to gather, read, and evaluate information;
- to move your paper from rough drafts to final draft;
- to prepare your works-cited list; and
- to proofread and edit the final copy you will turn in to your professor.

Creating a rough list of the tasks involved in preparing a research paper will reveal an important truth: Every task in life takes longer than you expect it will. Be realistic about the time it will take to write your paper. Hopefully this process will make it clear to you that if you wait until the night before the paper is due to begin your research, you won't be satisfied with the quality of the paper you'll be turning in.

Choosing a Topic

Some professors will give you a list of topics from which you may choose the one that most interests you. Others will assign each student a specific topic, and some professors will allow you to research and write about any subject that interests you. Try to choose a topic that truly engages your interest— ideally a topic you've always wanted to know more about but have not yet had the opportunity to spend any time researching. Choose a topic that will interest your readers as well, one that will teach them something they didn't know.

Consider surfing the Internet a bit to look for a subject that interests you. Or is there some topic you're studying in another course that you would like to learn more about? If you are writing a paper for an English class, check with your professor to see if a topic in history, psychology, biology, or marine science is acceptable. The research you do will enhance your understanding of the material you're studying in the other class while earning you a good grade in English.

Narrowing Your Topic

Once you have identified a topic that interests you, you need to think about the length of time you have available to work on the paper and the number of pages you are required to submit. One of your most important jobs will be to decide exactly what aspect of the topic you will research and what approach you will take to your subject. You will also need to find out how much information is available on your topic. If there are literally thousands of books and articles on your topic, that might be a clue that the topic you have chosen is too broad and needs to be narrowed down. On the other hand, if you find very few sources, you may need to consider broadening your topic or even choosing a different one.

Make sure you have chosen a topic that you can do justice to in the number of pages your instructor has assigned. It is better to analyze a small topic thoroughly than to cover a huge topic superficially.

Let's say you are interested in writing a paper dealing with horror movies. Could you fully discuss every conceivable aspect of horror movies in a double-spaced, typewritten, ten-page research paper? Of course not. It would, in fact, be difficult to cover all the aspects of horror movies in a single book. A more manageable topic might be "An Analysis of Gary Oldman's Portrayal of Count Dracula in Bram Stoker's Dracula."

Creating a Working Outline to Guide Your Research

Creating a working outline can be a useful step in your research process. Make a rough list of the topics you think you will discuss in the paper to guide your research. Deciding what you plan to discuss in the paper before you begin your research will help you avoid wasting time reading sources that will provide no useful information. This outline will undoubtedly change as you find new sources and decide what you will cover in your paper. A working outline will help you decide if the order in which you are discussing materials in your paper is logical and whether your paragraphs contain enough supporting details. It will also help you eliminate repetitive or irrelevant material from your paper. If information does not support your thesis, it probably does not belong in your paper. Time spent developing and analyzing your working outline will help you move through the research and writing processes more efficiently.

Creating a Working Bibliography

As you find sources in your library or on the Internet that you expect will provide useful information on your topic, type into your computer (or record on note cards) the bibliographic citation for each source that will appear in your works-cited list if you decide to quote, paraphrase, or summarize material from that source. This list is called a working bibliography, and it will eventually become your works-cited list.

Take the bibliographical information directly from the source to make sure that it is correct. If you have taken bibliographical information from a card catalog, online catalog, or index in your library, compare it with the information provided in your source to make sure your citation is accurate.

If information necessary for your citation (for example, the year of publication for a book entry) is missing in the source you are using but available in an index, card catalog, online catalog, or other source, place that information in square brackets in your citation: New York: Houghton, [1988].

Your working bibliography should be completed before you write the first draft of your paper so you will know how to do the parenthetical citations correctly as you incorporate your quotations, paraphrases, and summaries into the text of your paper. To format parenthetical citations, you will need to know if you are citing from two authors with the same last name or if you are citing from two or more works by the same author.

The most efficient method of creating a working bibliography is to type the bibliographic entries into a computer. As you locate sources that you expect will provide useful information, create the bibliographic citations exactly as they will appear in your works-cited or works-consulted list. You can also cut and paste citations from your sources into your working bibliography, but be sure to change this raw bibliographical data to MLA format.

Your working bibliography may contain additional information not necessary for the works-cited list. You might consider placing this information in angle brackets (< >) or parentheses to remind yourself later that this information does not belong in the final version of your citation. At the end of each citation, be sure to include the library call number for books, the Web address (URL) for Internet sources unless it is already part of the citation, and exactly where you found the information about this source in case you need to locate the source again at a later date. Be scrupulously accurate when recording Web addresses; the slightest error will mean that your computer will not be able to return to the Web site.

As you read your sources, check the footnotes, endnotes, parenthetical citations, and works-cited/consulted lists. Use the hypertext links in online sources. Each source you read is likely to lead you to other useful sources.

Your working bibliography will change as you delete sources that provided no useful information and add others that you intend to read. When you have finished writing the body of your paper, simply delete the unused sources and alphabetize those from which you quoted, paraphrased, or summarized information, and the working bibliography will become your works-cited list.

Another method is to write the bibliographic entries on note cards, which can be alphabetized easily when you are ready to type the entries into your computer. The cards for sources that did not provide useful information can be discarded. If you are using note cards for notes also, use a different color or size for the working bibliography.

You might prefer to create a handwritten list of sources. When you are ready to convert your working bibliography into your works-cited list, simply cross though sources you didn't cite, number the remaining entries in alphabetical order, and type them into your computer.

Your computer will alphabetize for you, but be sure to verify the ordering of the list before you submit it to your professor. Your computer is not getting the grade on the paper; you are.

Finding Sources in the Library

A tour of the library guided by a reference librarian or by your professor is one of the easiest ways to learn how the library at your school operates and what resources it provides to assist you with your research. Most libraries also provide maps, handouts, and Web sites designed to help you find what you need.

Professional reference librarians are trained in locating research materials of all kinds and will be happy to help you learn how to find the materials you need for your research paper. Don't expect the librarians to do your work for you, however. Remember that you will write many research papers during your college career, so you need to learn how to find sources yourself. If this is the first time you've researched a topic in your school's library, however, be sure to ask for help until you learn what resources are available and how to use them.

Using Card and Online Catalogs

Although some libraries still list their holdings in a card catalog, many others have computerized or online catalogs that can be accessed on the Internet through a library computer terminal or your personal computer. If your library has both a card and an online catalog, ask a librarian whether all available sources are listed in both catalogs. In some cases, older materials are listed in the card catalogs and only the most recent acquisitions are listed in the online catalog. Or your library may be in the process of transferring the data in the card catalog to the online catalog. Ask a librarian whether you need to check both catalogs.

Finding Books

If your school has a card catalog, you will find the books your library owns listed on bibliography cards stored in drawers. Sources are typically listed in three ways: by author, by title, and by subject.

Online catalogs can typically be searched by author, title, author/title, subject, keyword, or call numbers. You may limit your search by year of publication, language, format (book, journal, videotape, LP, CD, DVD, etc.), where you would expect to find the item (main collection, rare book collection, reserves, media collection, etc.). Look for a limit search key on your screen.

Once you have determined the call number of the book you need, you can find the book on the library shelves. If your library has closed stacks, you will need to present a call slip containing the call number to a librarian at the checkout desk, and the book will be located and brought to you.

Finding Reference Books

If the call number of a book begins with "Ref," you are looking at a reference book, which is typically shelved in a separate reference section of the library. Reference books cannot usually be checked out, so you must take notes from them in the library or photocopy the materials you need and read them later.

Finding Reserve Books and Journal Articles

Professors will often put a number of books and/or journal articles on reserve in the library so that all students in a particular class will have access to the materials. Reserve materials can be checked out for library use only or sometimes for overnight use. If your school has an online catalog, you can probably access the reserve lists for various professors through your computer. If not, ask to see the reserve lists at the checkout desk. Most online catalogs will tell you whether an item is available, checked out, or on reserve.

Finding Articles in Periodicals: Scholarly Journals, Popular Magazines, and Newspapers

Scholarly journals, popular magazines, and newspapers are typically found in three separate areas of the library. Recently published copies will be available in a current periodicals section. Older materials are generally found either in a separate bound periodicals section of your library, in the regular stacks, or on microfilm. Consult your library's periodicals list, which should be available in book form or through your school's online catalog or both. This guide to periodicals will tell you what scholarly journals, magazines, and newspapers your library subscribes to, when the library began receiving the subscriptions, any gaps in the subscriptions, and whether the material you need is located in the bound section, in the regular stacks, or on microfilm.

Using Reference Databases to Locate Materials in Scholarly Journals, Popular Magazines, Newspapers, and Other Sources

You will need to use reference databases to find materials in scholarly journals, popular magazines, newspapers, and other sources relevant to your topic. Reference databases may be in print, online, on CD-ROM, or on microform. Some of these databases may be freely used by anyone; others may be subscription databases available only to students and faculty of the university that pays for the subscription. Some databases give only citations, but the most useful databases will give citations, abstracts (paragraph-length summaries), and full-text reprints of research materials. Check your library's Web site to see which reference databases are available to you.

THE CITATIONS YOU FIND IN REFERENCE DATABASES ARE RAW MATERIALS FOR YOUR MLA-STYLE BIBLIOGRAPHY. ALTHOUGH THE DATABASE WILL GIVE YOU ALL THE INFORMATION YOU NEED TO CREATE YOUR MLA-STYLE CITATION, THE INFORMATION WILL NOT BE GIVEN IN THE SAME FORMAT YOU WILL BE EXPECTED TO USE ON YOUR WORKS-CITED PAGE. (IN CHAPTER 13 YOU WILL FIND MODEL CITATIONS FOR FULL-TEXT REPRINTS TAKEN FROM REFERENCE DATABASES.)

Online Reference Databases: A Few to Consider

- **America: History and Life**—gives citations and abstracts of articles published since 1964 in scholarly journals and books on topics relating to American and Canadian history from prehistory to modern times; no full-text reprints
- **Business NewsBank**—gives citations, abstracts, and some full-text reprints of articles related to business published in American newspapers
- **CQ (Congressional Quarterly) Researcher**—gives full-text reprints of articles on current events and social issues

- **EBSCOhost: MasterFILE Premier** and **EBSCOhost: Adademic Search Elite**—gives citations, abstracts, and some full-text reprints of articles from scholarly journals, popular magazines, newspapers, and other sources in the areas of social issues, science, business, humanities, literature, education, etc. (EBSCO is an acronym for Elton B. Stephens Company. Do not spell out EBSCO when you cite from this database.)

- **Electric Library**—gives citations and full-text reprints of articles from scholarly journals, magazines, newspapers, and books dealing with current events, social issues, popular culture, etc.

- **Gale Literature Resource Center**—gives full-text biographical information and critical evaluations of the works of thousands of authors

- **General Business File ASAP**—gives citations, abstracts, and some full-text reprints of articles published in scholarly journals, professional magazines, and trade publications covering topics related to business (finance, accounting, real estate, etc.); includes **Business Index** (indexes business related magazines and journals), **Company Profiles** (gives information on thousands of companies), and **Investext** (full-text financial analyst reports). (ASAP is an acronym for As Soon As Possible. Use ASAP when citing this database.)

- **General Reference Center**—gives citations, abstracts, and many full-text reprints of articles from popular magazines, newspapers, and reference books. (General Reference Center is an InfoTrac database.)

- **Health Reference Center**—gives citations, abstracts, and some full-text reprints of articles published in scholarly journals, popular magazines, and pamphlets in the fields of health and medicine (an InfoTrac database)

- **Historical Abstracts**—gives citations and abstracts of materials published since 1954 in scholarly journals and books on topics relating to world history (not including American and Canadian history); no full-text reprints

- **H. W. Wilson Select**—gives citations, abstracts, and some full-text reprints of articles from scholarly journals and popular magazines

- **InfoTrac: Expanded Academic ASAP**—gives citations, abstracts, and many full-text reprints of articles published in scholarly journals, popular magazines, and newspapers in fields such as literature, history, science, sociology, psychology, and anthropology. (This is one of a number of InfoTrac databases. ASAP is an acronym for As Soon As Possible and is included in the names of a number of InfoTrac databases. Do not spell ASAP out when citing material from this database.)

- **LEXIS-NEXIS Academic Universe**—gives citations, abstracts, and full-text reprints from scholarly journals, magazines, newspapers, and other sources in the areas of news, business and financial information, legal information, health and medical information, etc.

- **MLA International Bibliography**—gives citations for scholarly journal articles and books in literature and linguistics; no full-text reprints. (MLA is an acronym for Modern Language Association. You may use MLA when citing this database.)
- **NewsBank NewsFile Collection**—gives full-text reprints of articles published in American newspapers. (Older reprints may be available on microfiche.)
- **Oceanic Abstracts**—gives citations and abstracts of articles in scholarly journals in oceanography and marine science; no full-text reprints
- **ProQuest Direct**—gives citations and full-text reprints from scholarly journals, popular magazines, newspapers, and other sources related to a variety of vocational and technical subjects such as agriculture, computing, education, electronics, food service, health, hotel management, military, nursing, office systems, public safety, security, etc.
- **SIRS Knowledge Source**—gives citations and full-text reprints of articles published in scholarly journals, popular magazines, and newspapers; includes **SIRS Researcher**—full-text articles related to current events and social issues; **SIRS Government Reporter**—full-text historical documents and information by and about the U. S. government and its agencies; **SIRS Renaissance**—full-text articles related to the arts, literature, and the humanities. (SIRS is an acronym for Social Issues Resources Series. Use SIRS when citing this database.)
- **UMI Periodical Abstracts**—gives citations, abstracts, and some full-text reprints of articles from scholarly journals and popular magazines. (UMI is an acronym for University Microfilms International. Do not spell UMI out when citing this database.)

Print Periodical Indexes: A Few to Consider

- **New York Times Index**—lists articles and reviews published in the New York Times newspaper
- **Reader's Guide to Periodical Literature**—gives citations for articles in popular magazines and in some scholarly journals
- **SIRS (Social Issues Resources Series)**—a loose-leaf print collection of full-text articles reprinted from American magazines and newspapers; each volume or series of volumes covers a specific topic such as Women, AIDS, Education, and Health; for recent materials consult the online version of this database

Free Databases on the Web: A Few to Consider

- **AGRICOLA (Agricultural Online Access)** <http://www.nal.usda.gov/ag98/english/index-basic.html>—gives citations for journal articles, reports, and books dealing with agriculture and related fields

- **American Universities** <http://www.clas.ufl.edu/CLAS/ american-universities.html> — provides links to home pages of an alphabetical list of American universities

- **ERIC** (**Educational Resources Information Center**) <http://ericae.net/ scripts/ewiz/amain2.asp> or <http://ericir.syr.edu/Eric/> — includes **RIE** (**Resources in Education**), which indexes educational documents and conference presentations and **CIJE** (**Current Index to Journals in Education**), which indexes scholarly journal articles in the fields of education, physical education, sports, etc.; full-text reprints may be available on microfiche for RIE materials

- **Federal Web Locator** <http://www.infoctr.edu/fwl/> — useful for locating the Web sites of federal agencies

- **Government Information Xchange** <http://www.info.gov> — a service provided by the General Services Administration (GSA) for locating information related to the federal government; try the Federal Directory link

- **Lakewood Public Library's Selection of Ready Reference Web Sites** <www.lkwdpl.org/readref.htm> — provides links to a variety of Web sites relating to philosophy, psychology, religion, social sciences, languages, natural sciences, mathematics, technology, the arts, literature, rhetoric, geography, history, etc.

- **LibraryHQ Site Source** <http://www.libraryhq.com/> — provides a searchable database of useful Web sites

- **PubMed** <http://www.ncbi.nlm.nih.gov/PubMed/> — gives citations and abstracts for journals and books in medicine and related fields

- **GPO** (**Government Printing Office**) **Access** <http://www.access.gpo.gov/ su_docs> — use to access numerous databases to search for government documents

- **THOMAS: Legislative Information on the Internet** <http:// thomas.loc .gov> — use to locate information related to the legislative branch of the federal government

- **Winsor School's Ready-Reference Using the Internet** <http://winsor.edu/ library/rref.htm> — gives links to information on a variety of topics organized from A to Z; maintained by the Winsor School, Boston, MA

Finding Additional Sources Available in Most Libraries

You will also find rare books, government publications, pamphlet files, and audiovisual materials of various types in most libraries. Ask a librarian where these materials are located.

Considering an Interlibrary Loan

If your library does not own a book, pamphlet, government document, scholarly journal, magazine, or newspaper article you need and the material cannot be accessed through the full-text reference databases, ask a librarian how long it will take to get the material from another library though the interlibrary loan process.

Searching for Sources on the Internet

The World Wide Web is a giant network of hypertext connections to literally millions of electronic sites featuring texts, graphics, and sounds. Using a Web browser (such as Netscape Navigator, Netscape Communicator, or Microsoft Internet Explorer) and a search engine that indexes Web sites (such as Yahoo!, AltaVista, Excite, GoTo, Lycos, HotBot, WebCrawler, or Infoseek), try a keyword search. Many search engines can be accessed by typing <http://www.nameofsearchengine.com> into the dialog box at the top of your Web browser screen and hitting enter. For example, to get to AltaVista, simply type <http://www.altavista.com>, and hit enter. To access GoTo, type <http://goto.com>, and hit enter.

Angle brackets < > typed around an electronic address mean that all the characters typed between them should be considered a single unit with no spaces between the characters. If you accidentally type a space or mistype a character in a Web address, your browser will not find the address. Do not type the angle brackets in the dialog box of your Web browser.

The search engine's help menu will give you timesaving tips on searching effectively. Be as specific as possible when doing a keyword search; otherwise, you will access numerous irrelevant sites and waste time. Even better is an exact phrase search. Type quotation marks around a phrase you wish to find information on (for example: "female body image"). If you make a mistake, the search engine screen will give you advice about what to do to make your search more effective.

Using Boolean Operators: AND, OR, NOT, NEAR

Use the Boolean operators AND, OR, NOT, or NEAR to link words in a search. When you link terms with AND (anorexia AND bulimia), both terms must be present in the title for a successful hit; therefore, you are narrowing your search. Terms linked with OR (anorexia OR bulimia) will expand your search to include titles containing both or just one of the terms you have listed. Use NOT to eliminate any documents that contain the word typed after NOT (anorexia NOT bulimia). Some search engines allow you to use the word NEAR to locate documents in which two key terms appear close together. The plus and minus signs are generally equivalent to the terms AND and NOT (anorexia +bulimia; anorexia −bulimia).

Using Wild Cards or Truncation Symbols in a Search

Be sure to check the help menu of whatever search engine you are using to see what types of operators and truncation symbols it requires. Also bear in mind that truncation symbols may work only in advanced searches. Your search engine may allow you to use an asterisk * to locate documents containing words beginning with specified letters. For example, trou* would find documents whose titles contain words such as troubadour, troupe, trousseau, and trout. The asterisk is also useful for finding sources with non-American spellings in their titles (for example, hon*r should give you honor and honour; Ka*mir should give you Kazmir and Kashmir).

If you can't remember how to spell a keyword or an author's name, your search engine may allow you to type a question mark (?) or some other symbol, such as a dollar sign ($), in place of the letters you're unsure of. Thus Brown? should give you citations for Brown, Browne, and Browning, etc.

Don't forget to bookmark useful sites so you can easily find them again. Bear in mind when surfing the Net that a site you find on Monday may be unavailable by Tuesday or the materials on the site may have been revised or updated. Therefore, to be safe, print a hard copy of any material you think will provide useful information. Add the appropriate MLA-style citation for each site you believe will be useful to your working bibliography while you have the material on your computer screen so you can be sure you have all the information you will need if you decide later to quote, paraphrase, or summarize material from that site.

Bear in mind also that some Internet sites, such as e-mail discussion groups and online chat rooms, may not provide the type of information you would want to cite in a research paper although they might provide useful links to more appropriate sources.

Evaluating Research Sources

My grandmother always believed everything she read in the local newspaper. She was sure that if it had been printed in a newspaper published in her hometown, it just had to be true. But if you walked into your local grocery store and saw a headline in a tabloid newspaper reading "Julia Roberts Abducted by Aliens," would you believe the article just because it was in print? You're intelligent enough to know that some disreputable newspapers make huge profits by printing exaggerations, half-truths, and just plain lies—hoping nobody will bother to sue them.

Let the Researcher Beware

The famous axiom *caveat emptor* means "let the buyer beware." A good rule of thumb in writing research papers is "Believe nothing you hear and only half of what you read."

One of your most important jobs as a researcher is to evaluate the material you read and determine what is reliable information worthy to be quoted, paraphrased, or summarized in your paper and what is outdated, biased, or downright incorrect.

Print Sources versus Internet Sources

Before a scholarly book is published by a reputable publisher, it has typically been read and evaluated by expert consultants (called peer reviewers) who have assured the publisher that the material in the book is current, well researched, and reliable. Articles appearing in scholarly journals go through a similar rigorous peer review process and normally will not be published unless they meet the high standards of the editorial staff of the journal. Professional editors review articles written for popular magazines, newsmagazines, and newspapers, verifying the accuracy of the information presented and making sure that libelous information is not published.

On the other hand, anyone from a reputable scholar to a Web-savvy third grader can publish anything on the Internet. Information presented as part of a scholarly Web site maintained by expert researchers on the staff of a reputable university might prove more current than any information to be found in books or journals published on the same topic. Many authors maintain Web sites so that their readers can constantly access updated information on a particular subject. You might find excellent research materials in an online, peer-reviewed scholarly journal. But you might also find online magazines and journals that publish any material submitted to them regardless of its accuracy or bias. You can find extremely liberal online magazines as well as extremely conservative magazines and just about anything in between.

Evaluating Print Sources

If a scholarly book has been published by a reputable publishing house, odds are good that it is a reliable source. But then again, not much in life is certain. If you are not sure about whether you should use information from a particular book, evaluate it using the print or online versions of Book Review Index or Book Review Digest. Through these sources you can get a feel for the consensus among expert reviewers on the validity of the ideas presented in the book.

If an article has been published in a peer-reviewed scholarly journal, you can be relatively sure that it contains reliable information. But always use your common sense to weigh what you are reading against what you are finding in your other sources. If the ideas in one article seem to contradict information in many of your other sources, consider discussing the source with your professor before you use information from it as the basis of your paper. In the area of literary criticism, for example, there are many interpretations of various literary works. Some may ring true to you, whereas others may seem totally unreasonable or just the opposite of what you think the work means. Ultimately you must decide what information from your sources is valid enough to be incorporated into your paper.

Evaluating Internet Sources

Ask yourself the following questions when you are evaluating any source, but especially an Internet source:

(1) Author's credentials

- Who wrote this information, and what are this writer's credentials?
- What is the writer's position or title?
- For whom does this writer work?
- To whom is this writer loyal?
- What is this writer's purpose in making this information available on the Web?
- Does the site include an e-mail or postal address so you can contact the author and ask questions?
- Is the author of this site trying to persuade you to buy something, to donate money to a particular organization, or to change your thinking or behavior in some way that would benefit the writer or the organization for which he or she works?
- Is the author a distinguished professor currently teaching political science courses at Harvard University who has published numerous scholarly journal articles and books on the Vietnam War?
- Or is the writer a veteran of the Vietnam War whose life was forever changed when he stepped on a mine that blew his legs off? Although the war veteran might have firsthand knowledge of certain events, might his version of the reality of the war be biased by his firmly held belief that American soldiers had no business fighting in Vietnam in the first place?
- Is the author presenting an unbiased, objective account of events? Or does this writer have a personal, political, or commercial agenda? Is the author's bias cleverly hidden or clearly obvious?

If no author is given, you have no way to evaluate the credentials or credibility of the writer. Think twice about citing information from such a site.

(2) Timeliness

- How current is this information?
- When was this Web site created?
- When was the information it contains updated?
- Could new information have been discovered since this Web site was updated?

In many fields, what is true on Monday has been disproved by Friday. If you are researching a scientific, medical, business, or technological topic, you should be careful to use the most current information available to you.

Even in the field of literary analysis, ideas about authors and interpretations of their works change. Although a critical interpretation of Prince Hamlet of Denmark, Shakespeare's most famous tragic hero, might be as accurate today as when it was written fifty years ago, in other cases, opinions and interpretations once accepted now seem outdated or absurd. For example, when Herman Melville first published <u>Moby Dick</u>, one reviewer described the book as "trash." Today Melville is considered a brilliant symbolist, and <u>Moby Dick</u> is considered one of the greatest American novels.

Because critical opinions of both authors and literary works change from decade to decade, you might want to think twice about quoting a critic who wrote his or her opinions fifty years ago unless you are certain that the critic's ideas are still valid and current.

(3) Credibility

- Can the information on the Web site be verified?
- Is there a list of works cited or consulted so that you can evaluate the sources from which the author took his or her information?
- Does the site include hypertext links to other sources through which the information presented on the site can be verified and additional information on the subject can be found?

Note the Last Three Letters of the Domain Name in the Web Address

.com	a commercial site	.net	a network management site
.edu	an educational site	.org	a nonprofit organization site
.gov	a county, state, or federal government site	.ca	a Canadian site
.mil	a military site	.au	an Australian site

Commercial Sites: .com

Information found on commercial sites may be reliable or may simply be designed to sell you the goods that can be ordered through the site.

On amazon.com, for example, you can access not only information about the availability and price of a book, CD, or videotaped movie you might wish to purchase, but also reviews written by Internet surfers just like you who have read the book, listened to the CD, or seen the movie. However, are the reviews you are reading as authoritative as a book review published in the New York Times Book Review, a CD review written by a professional columnist for Musician Magazine or Rolling Stone, or a movie review written by Roger Ebert for publication in the Chicago Sun-Times or Roger Ebert's Movie Home Companion?

Who wrote what you're reading? Is the author an expert on this subject? You'd be better advised to quote from well-known movie critic Roger Ebert's analysis than from an analysis written by a fellow Internet surfer who might be a professional house painter who enjoys watching movies in his spare time.

On the other hand, you can find highly useful information on reputable commercial sites such as those maintained by well-known magazines such as Time and Newsweek or prestigious newspapers such as the New York Times, the Los Angeles Times, and the Washington Post.

Educational Sites: .edu

On educational sites, you might find scholarly projects created by knowledgeable professors who have published extensively in their fields of expertise and will provide you with highly reliable research materials.

Professors often maintain Web sites to keep students in a particular class informed about assignments and due dates for papers. They often post model papers written by themselves, by graduate assistants, or by former students to their Web sites to help their current students better understand what is expected in the papers they are writing for the class.

Don't assume, however, that professors post only excellent work to their Web pages. Many professors believe students learn how to write a good paper more effectively if they study flawed model papers. Thus professors are just as likely to post examples of what not to do in a good paper as to post examples of ideal papers. If you're not hearing the class discussions, can you tell the difference between an ideal model paper and one that would have received a low or failing grade? Are you sure?

You might also be accessing a site created by a first-year graduate student instructor rather than by an experienced graduate instructor or professor.

Because anyone can create a personal page on the Internet—even a child — you might be accessing a Web page created by a student as part of a class project or just for the fun of the experience. Can you tell if the information you're reading was posted by a senior marine science major who has done extensive research on water quality in local marshes or by a student in grammar, middle, or high school who is discussing a class assignment with classmates through the Internet?

Carefully evaluate the information you're reading before accepting it as reliable.

Government Sites: .gov

Information taken from sites maintained by city, county, state, or federal agencies is likely to be current, well researched, and highly reliable, but as always, compare what you are reading with information you are finding in your other sources and double-check anything that does not seem credible.

Nonprofit Organizational Sites: .org

Does the organization sponsoring this site have a political agenda?

If you are reading information posted on the Web site of the National Rifle Association, an organization adamantly opposed to gun regulation, can you expect to find a fair representation of the position of those who favor gun regulations? Or if you are reading information posted on a PETA (People for the Ethical Treatment of Animals) sponsored site, would you expect the authors to support the use of live animals in scientific research? Does this site present information fairly and objectively? Does it present all sides of the issues under discussion?

A Source Evaluation Checklist

Look for the following indicators of an unreliable Web site:

- No author is identified. Therefore, you have no way of checking out the credentials or possible biases of the writer.
- There is no evidence that the information presented has been reviewed and established as reliable by some sort of peer review process.
- You notice errors of fact. When you are doing research, you will see some basic information repeated from source to source whereas other information will be specific to one particular source. If the source you are reading does not correctly present the information you know to be true, it is reasonable to assume that the new information on this site may be unreliable.
- No date of posting or updating is given. Thus there is no way for you to evaluate whether the information given on the site is current or out-of-date.

- The author's statements are not supported by convincing evidence or specific details.

- Opposing viewpoints are not acknowledged or addressed.

- The writer's tone is highly emotional (angry, spiteful, clearly biased) rather than calm and reasonable.

- The information presented seems exaggerated.

- No sources or hypertext links are given, so you have no way of checking the accuracy of any statistics presented on the site. For all you know, the author could be making these numbers up.

- The writing on the Web site is sloppy. Sentences may be unclear or awkward. You notice misspelled words, incorrect grammar, and punctuation errors. Educated writers tend to be conscientious enough to revise awkward or unclear sentences and to check the accuracy of their spelling, grammar, and punctuation. If a writer has not bothered to check these aspects of the writing, how likely is it that he or she has checked the accuracy of the facts and opinions presented on the site?

Taking Notes

Copy directly quoted material exactly as it will appear in your paper if you decide to use it. Copy it in quotation marks with brackets used to specify any clarifications or changes you made in the text and with bracketed ellipses used to indicate any omissions not already obvious to your reader.

Photocopy or print out from your computer as much of the material you will read as possible so you can annotate what you read and so you will have your sources available to check the accuracy of your quotations, paraphrases, and summaries as you incorporate them into the text of your first or later drafts.

Suppose you find a book or scholarly journal article you believe will contain just the information you need to incorporate into your paper. Photocopy the relevant pages in the book or article so that you can take them home, write sidebar annotations on them, and highlight useful information.

> DO NOT WRITE ON MATERIAL THAT BELONGS TO THE LIBRARY.

Just in case the title, author, or page numbers are cut off of the pages when you photocopy from a source, write the bibliographical citation for the source on the first page of your photocopy before you allow the original version to leave your hands.

The most important thing to remember when you take notes from your sources is that you must clearly distinguish between quoted, paraphrased, and summarized material that must be documented in your paper and ideas that do not require documentation because they are considered general knowledge about that subject. As you do your research, you will also have original ideas about the subject that you will want to remember later when you write your first draft. Keep a list of your own ideas handwritten on note cards or on sheets of paper, or typed into your computer so that you can cut and paste them later.

In the margin beside each piece of information you write, type, or download into your notes, write or type some sort of letter, symbol, or word that will tell you later whether the material recorded there is

- a direct quotation (DQ),
- a paraphrase (P),
- a summary (S),
- general knowledge information (G),
- or your own original idea (M, or type angle brackets around your own ideas).

When you are ready to begin taking notes from your photocopied source, sit down at your computer and type the bibliographic citation for that particular source onto the top of your page. As you read, type the page number from your source at the left margin so you will know later exactly what page in the source you took the notes from. When you have finished taking notes on that source, have your computer number and print the pages (just in case the hard drive on your computer or your backup disk fails before your paper is turned in). Always print out your work to be safe. Then clip your notes to the top of your photocopy of the original materials. Later, when you are writing your first draft, your photocopy will allow you to check the accuracy of your quotations, paraphrases, and summaries by comparing what you have written to the material in your original sources.

Typing or downloading materials you might want to quote, paraphrase, or summarize later into your computerized notes as you do your research will also allow you to cut and paste later, saving you the time it would take to re-type handwritten materials from sheets of paper or note cards.

CHAPTER 4

Writing and Revising Your Paper

Writing the Paper

Read through all your notes right before you begin your rough draft so the material will be fresh in your memory, and highlight things you might want to incorporate into your text. If you have kept a separate list of ideas that came to you as you did your research, those ideas will be the most important ideas expressed in your paper. **Avoid using an excessive number of quotations, paraphrases, and summaries in your paper.** Although there is no hard and fast rule on this, two or three citations per page of text should be about right. Most of the paper should be your own analysis of the subject expressed in your own words.

Preparing a Final Outline for Your Paper

If your professor requires you to turn in an outline with your paper, simply convert your working outline into the format required by your professor.

Preparing a Topic Outline

A topic outline consists of parallel words or phrases and usually follows a format such as the one described here. Generally if you have an A in such an outline, you should also have a B, and so on.

Caitlin Crawford-Lamb

Dr. Nelljean Rice

English 150: 10:00 TTH

9 December 1999

Title: Finding Shelter in the Storm: The Turbulent Influence of Society on the Body Image of Adolescent Girls

Thesis: Adolescent females are becoming more and more obsessed with body image issues, an obsession that often leads to emo-

tional instability and eating disorders such as anorexia and
bulimia.

   I. Definition of body image

      A. Healthy body image

      B. Unhealthy body image

  II. Societal influences on body image

      A. External influences

         1. Female gender role

            a. Overfeminized role

            b. Beauty defining worth

         2. "Lookism"

            a. Media input

            b. Cultural input

         3. Socialization of food worth

            a. Weight as a reference point

            b. Search for emotional nourishment

      B. Peer group influences

         1. Concern over weight as a unifying force

         2. Forum to gain acceptance and support from peers

 III. Physical consequences of unhealthy body image

      A. Anorexia nervosa

      B. Bulimia

Preparing a Sentence Outline

A sentence outline follows the same basic format as a topic outline. Simply substitute sentences for the words or phrases used in a topic outline.

Preparing a Controlling Sentence Outline

A simple way to create a final outline is to list the thesis for the paper, the topic sentences for each paragraph, and the conclusion sentence.

Thesis

The **thesis** is the controlling sentence for the entire paper. It typically explains what you will analyze, prove, or discuss in your paper. Although in some types of writing the thesis can be implied, it is usually stated near or at the end of the first paragraph.

Topic Sentence

A **topic sentence** is the controlling sentence for a particular paragraph within the essay. In certain types of writing, paragraphs have implied topic sentences. If this is the case, simply create for your outline the topic sentences that would be there if the paragraphs had them.

Conclusion Sentence

A **conclusion sentence** is the controlling sentence of the last paragraph of your essay. Often it is the first or last sentence in your concluding paragraph. It may restate the thesis in a slightly different way, may summarize what has been said in the essay, or may emphasize a final important idea you want to leave with your reader. The conclusion sentence brings a sense of completion to your essay.

A controlling sentence outline will help you make sure

- that all the information contained in your paper supports the thesis,
- that each of your paragraphs is unified (covers a single idea),
- that your essay doesn't just stop abruptly, but rather has a sense of closure, and
- that you are presenting the information in your essay in a logical pattern.

(See William Files's controlling sentence outline in chapter 7.)

```
Thesis Statement:

Topic Sentence for Body Paragraph 1:

Topic Sentence for Body Paragraph 2:

Topic Sentence for Body Paragraph 3:

Topic Sentence for Body Paragraph 4:

Conclusion Sentence:
```

Preparing Your Works-Cited Page

Delete from your working bibliography any sources that provided no useful information. Alphabetize your sources by the authors' last names or, if no author was given, by the title (excluding *A, An,* and *The*). Your works-cited list is the last page of your paper and should be numbered as part of your text. Remember to double-space everything on your works-cited page.

Revising Your Paper

When you have finished your first draft, revise, revise, revise, and then revise again. Let the paper sit overnight or, better still, for a day or two so you can read it with fresh eyes to look for problems.

Remember that your professor is looking for a clear presentation of your own analysis of the subject you have researched, not just a series of direct quotations, paraphrases, and summaries cut and pasted from your sources.

Reread the assignment sheets to see if you have forgotten anything you were required to include.

If your professor listed the criteria by which your paper will be evaluated, read them again and ask yourself if you have fulfilled your professor's expectations and formatting requirements.

Although the most important aspect of any paper is what you say in it (the content), your grade will most likely suffer if what you are trying to say is not clear to your reader. Excessively long or complicated sentences and mechanical, grammatical, punctuation, spelling, and typographical errors are not only distracting but annoying to any reader, but especially to a reader as well educated as your professor. In addition, such errors suggest that you are not conscientious about your work. When you see this sort of sloppiness in a source, it immediately suggests that you may not be able to rely on the accuracy of the research being presented. You want your reader to rely on the accuracy of your research; therefore, the presentation of your research is an important aspect of your paper.

Read your paper into a tape recorder and listen to it so you can try to spot paragraphs that seem illogically organized or sentences that need clarification.

If you are having trouble with the paper, set up an appointment for a conference with your professor.

If your university provides a writing center or lab, make use of the help to be found there. If allowed by your professor, get classmates, friends, or relatives to read the paper and give you feedback. However, be sure to inform your professor about any help you received in writing the paper.

A Revision Checklist

- Is your paper interesting? Will others enjoy reading it?

- Will your paper teach your readers something they might not have known before about this subject, or are you just rehashing well-known information?

- Have you clearly stated or implied the thesis (main point/controlling idea) of your paper?

- Have you given enough supporting information to prove your thesis?

- Are the ideas presented in your paper logically organized?

- Does each paragraph in your paper have a clearly stated or implied topic (controlling) sentence?

- Are your paragraphs **unified?** Does everything in each paragraph specifically relate to the stated or implied topic sentence?

- Is the material in each paragraph **coherent?** Is there a logical reason for the order in which the sentences are presented? Did you use enough transitional words and phrases to clarify the relationships of the ideas to each other?

- Is your paper **unified?** Does everything in the paper specifically relate to the stated or implied thesis (controlling idea for the entire paper)?

- Is your paper **coherent?** Is there a logical reason for the order in which the paragraphs are presented? Did you use enough transitional words and phrases to clarify the relationships of the paragraphs to each other?

- Does your essay just stop, or does the concluding paragraph leave your reader with a sense of closure?

- Have you clearly identified and correctly documented all material taken from your sources?

- Have you eliminated any mechanical, grammatical, punctuation, spelling, or typographical errors?

CHAPTER 5

Formatting Your Paper

Use one-inch top, bottom, left, and right margins.

Double-space everything in your paper including the quotations, the end-note page if you have one, and the works-cited page.

Use good quality white 8½-by-11-inch paper, and type or print only on one side.

Use a type size large enough to be easy to read, and make sure the print is not too light. A good choice in most fonts is 12-point type. Choose a font that looks professional and businesslike. Times New Roman, Arial, Courier, and Helvetica are good choices.

Indent all paragraphs one-half inch (on a computer) or five spaces (on a typewriter) from the left margin.

Indent all quotations that take up five or more lines when typed into your paper one inch (on a computer) or ten spaces (on a typewriter) from the left margin. Long quotations such as these are called block (or set off) quotations.

Justify your lines only to the left margin, not to both margins.

Type your last name and the page number (Smith 4) in the top right corner of all pages beginning with the outline if you are required to submit one. This can be done on your computer as a **header,** which will appear one-half inch from the top of each page. You will find the header option under the View menu in most word-processing programs.

If your instructor does not require a title page, type the following information flush left and double-spaced beginning one inch from the top of the first page of your paper:

Your name	Jerome C. Smith
Your professor's name	Professor Jacobson
The course name: the time your class meets	English 102: 9:30 MWF
The day, month, and year your paper is due	15 January 2000

If your professor prefers a title page, center your title (not underlined, not in quotation marks, not in bold or italics) on a separate page. Next center your name, your professor's name, the class name, number, and time, and the paper's due date in a double-spaced list below the title.

If your professor requires an outline at the beginning of your paper, type the four-line heading on both the outline page and the first page of your paper and begin the last name and page number header (Smith 1) on the first page of the outline.

Double-space after the four-line heading and center your title on the first page of the text of your paper.

Use a colon and one space to separate your title from your subtitle.

Capitalize the first and last words of your title and subtitle and all other words with the exception of

- articles (*a, an, the*),
- prepositions (*in, on, to, under, between, over, through*),
- the seven coordinating conjunctions (FANBOYS: *for, and, nor, but, or, yet, so*), and
- the word *to* used in infinitives (*to* see, *to* run, *to* jump, etc.).

Do not underline or place your title in quotation marks, bold, italics, or all capital letters. Do not type a period after your title.

Remember that the purpose of your title is to tell your reader exactly what you will discuss in your paper. It should be very specific, fairly brief, and a phrase or a combination of words and phrases separated by a colon. With rare exceptions, your title should not be a sentence.

After your title, double-space and begin the text of your paper.

If you use an endnote page, number it as part of your text, and place it after the last page of the body of your paper and immediately before the works-cited list. (See chapter 15 for information on how to format endnotes.)

The works-cited list is the last page of your paper and should be numbered as part of your text. Center the title **Works Cited** or **Works Consulted** (not underlined, not in quotation marks, and not in bold or italics) one inch from the top of your page. Double-space after the title and list your citations in alphabetical order using a hanging indent: first line flush with the left margin; all subsequent lines in the same entry indented one-half inch (on a computer) or five spaces (on a typewriter) from the left margin.

Use the hanging indent option on your computer rather than the tab function to create a hanging indent. You will find the hanging indent option under Format/Paragraph/Indents and Spacing/Special menus in most word-processing programs. (See page 61 for more information on how to create a hanging indent.)

CHAPTER 6

Sample General Topic Research Paper

By Jessica Lynn Piezzo

Each student in Jessica Piezzo's English 101 class researched a person involved in the Salem witchcraft trials in Salem Village, Massachusetts, in 1692. Some students chose to write about one of the supposedly "afflicted" girls who made the accusations. Others wrote about the judges who sent those unfortunate enough to be convicted to their deaths. Jessica chose to discover what historians had to say about Sarah Good, one of the first three women accused of practicing witchcraft in Salem Village and the only one of those three to hang for her supposed allegiance to the Devil. Jessica was interested in finding out whether Sarah Good was given a fair trial and why she was convicted and condemned to death. Jessica later presented the results of her research during an on-campus conference held at her university featuring presentations by students and faculty.

> NOTE: MLA DOES NOT REQUIRE YOU TO FORMAT YOUR THESIS, TOPIC SENTENCES, AND CONCLUSION SENTENCE IN BOLD. IN THIS TEXT, BOLD IS USED SIMPLY TO HELP YOU LOCATE THE CONTROLLING SENTENCES IN THE MODEL STUDENT ESSAYS.

Piezzo 1

Jessica Lynn Piezzo

Professor Schwartz

English 101: 9:30 MWF

18 February 2000

The Story of Sarah Good: Guilty or Innocent?

Thesis: Although the court sentenced Sarah Good to death, she

maintained her innocence, and it seems clear that she was

falsely accused of being a witch.

I. Reasons for the accusations of witchcraft in Salem

    A. Dr. Griggs's unfortunate diagnosis

    B. Bruce Watson's theory

        1. Religious factors

        2. Political factors

        3. Economic factors

        4. Social factors

    C. Mary Beth Norton's theory

        1. Different situation than most other cases

        2. Fear of Indian attacks

II. Many lives destroyed

    A. 180 accused

    B. 144 arrested

Piezzo 2

    C. Giles Cory pressed to death

    D. Nineteen men and women hanged

    E. Six died in prison

III. Sarah's poverty a factor

    A. Cheated out of inheritance

    B. Left in debt after first husband's death

    C. Land confiscated to pay first husband's debts

    D. Married second husband, a ne'er-do-well

    E. Reduced to begging

IV. Tituba's false confession

    A. Sarah Good accused

    B. Sarah Osborne accused

V. Good's bad temper a factor

    A. Afflicted girls testified against her

    B. Disgruntled neighbors testified against her

    C. Husband testified against her

VI. Good's five-year-old daughter helped convict her

    A. Dorcas arrested, questioned, and imprisoned

    B. Dorcas accused mother

    C. Dorcas became mentally unstable

VII. Trial not fair

    A. Records show Hathorne's bias

    B. Good maintained innocence

VIII. Spectral evidence used against her

    A. Elizabeth Hubbard's accusation

    B. Constable's testimony

IX. Some evidence against Good proved false

    A. Broken knife incident

    B. Court ignored problem

X. Good defiant to the end

    A. Maintained innocence in last moments

    B. Irony of last words

XI. Reasons for Good's conviction

    A. Bad temper

    B. Poverty

    C. Powerlessness

Use one-inch top,
bottom, and right
margins.

Type your name,
your professor's
name, class name
and time, and the
paper due date
at the top left
margin of the
first page of your
outline and on
the first page of
the text of your
paper.

Your last name
and page number
should be a
header appearing
one-half inch
from the top of
every page in your
paper.

Jessica Lynn Piezzo

Professor Schwartz

English 101: 9:30 MWF

18 February 2000

The Story of Sarah Good: Guilty or Innocent?

Centered title
explains exactly
what will be
discussed in the
paper.

Jessica gives a
brief overview
of events that
occurred and
some possible
causes of the
Salem witch
trials.

1   The Salem Witch Trials began in the middle of

January 1692 when several young girls, including the daughter

and niece of Reverend Samuel Parris, began having bizarre

fits and were diagnosed by a local doctor as being bewitched.

Many of the "afflicted" girls were associated with prominent

families in Salem Village (now Danvers), Massachusetts. The

girls' inexplicable behavior and Dr. Griggs's unfortunate

diagnosis ultimately triggered the mass outbreak of witch

hysteria in Salem Village, which remains the most famous

incident of its kind in American history. Bruce Watson notes

that religious, political, economic, and social issues were

all important factors in the cause of this outbreak. Mary

Beth Norton, a professor of history at Cornell University,

notes that previous accusations of witchcraft in the New

England area targeted what she terms a few and never more

No page citation
is given for
Watson because
Jessica refers to
his article as a
whole.

The first time
you cite from an
author, give
the full name.
Thereafter, give
only the last
name.

Summary of
Norton's theory.
Author's name
is given at the
beginning, and
the page reference
is typed in paren-
theses before the
period of the last
sentence in the
summary.

Piezzo 2

than a dozen of "'the usual suspects'"--people who had long

been suspected by their neighbors of practicing witchcraft.

However, in Salem Village and the surrounding towns, hundreds

of people were accused, and although some of those accused--

Sarah Good and Sarah Osborne, for example--were "'the usual

suspects,'" many were respected individuals who had never

been suspected of any witch-like behavior before. She be-

lieves the hysteria may be explained by fear of the Indian

attacks that seemed to be moving closer and closer to Salem

Village at the time. One attack occurred only twenty miles

from Salem while the trials were being held. Many believed

that the devil and his minions were aiding the Indians;

therefore, anyone consorting with the devil at that partic-

MLA does not require page references for electronic sources with no page numbers given. Jessica's instructor, however, was checking her citations for accuracy and asked her to cite page numbers of the Web site printouts turned in with her paper.

ular historical moment would have been seen as a threat to

the survival of the village (9). **The tragic events that took**

Topic sentence for paragraph 1.

place in 1692 would destroy many lives--including Sarah

2 **Good's--and change Salem Village forever.**

The first formal accusations of witchcraft were made

General knowledge information available uncited in many sources may be presented in the student's own words without citing a source.

on February 29, 1692, and the last trials resulting from

those accusations occurred in May of 1693. Norton notes that

documented accusations against 180 people survive, but it
is likely that many others were accused as well. At least
144 inhabitants (38 men and 106 women) were arrested and
spent a considerable length of time in extremely harsh--in
some cases lethal--prison conditions (4). An eighty-year-old
man named Giles Cory was pressed (crushed) to death by heavy
stones because he refused to enter a plea, apparently hoping
to prevent his property from being confiscated. (The property
of condemned people was forfeited to the state, and Cory did
not want his children to lose their inheritance.) Six people
died in prison (three women, one man, and two infants), and
fourteen women and five men were hanged from a large tree on
Gallows Hill. One of the nineteen executed was Sarah Good.

Although the court sentenced Sarah Good to death, she
maintained her innocence throughout her trial, and it seems
clear that she was falsely accused of being a witch.

> Thesis statement explains what Jessica intends to prove in essay.

3   **Sarah Good's poverty was one of the factors that led to**
her tragic end. She was the daughter of a wealthy innkeeper
named John Solart. After he drowned himself in 1672, an
estate of approximately five hundred pounds was divided among

> Topic sentence for paragraph 3.

Piezzo 4

his wife and his two sons. His seven daughters were not to

receive their shares of the estate until they came of age.

Mrs. Solart, however, soon remarried, and her inheritance and

the shares destined for her daughters were turned over to

the control of her new husband. As a result, Sarah and her

sisters never saw their shares of the inheritance. When

Sarah's first husband, Daniel Poole, died, he left her

nothing but debts. Those debts were left to be paid by Sarah

and her second husband, William Good, by all accounts a

ne'er-do-well. They were forced to forfeit most of their land

to pay off Poole's debts and then sold the rest to pay their

living expenses. Katherine Sutcliffe explains that by the

1690s, Sarah, her husband, and their daughter were homeless

and "reduced to begging for work, food, and shelter from

[their] neighbors [. . .]" (1).

4   An Indian woman from Barbados named Tituba (a slave be-

longing to Rev. Samuel Parris), Sarah Good, and Sarah Osborne

were the first three women accused of practicing witchcraft

by the afflicted girls. After maintaining her innocence for

some time, Tituba eventually confessed to being a witch and

Jessica summarizes general background information about Sarah Good. Because this information is available uncited in many sources, Jessica can summarize it in her own words without giving a source.

Pronoun *her* in the source changed in square brackets to *their*. Bracketed ellipsis indicates that words after "neighbors" were omitted.

Piezzo 5

identified Sarah Good and Sarah Osborne as also being witches.

(Later Tituba claimed that her confession had been false--

beaten out of her by her master, Rev. Samuel Parris.) **Because**   Topic sentence for
                                                                     paragraph 4.

of Tituba's false confession, Sarah Good was one of the first

women actually brought to trial.

5   **Sarah's bad temper helped convict her of witchcraft.** She   Topic sentence for
                                                                         paragraph 5.

Paraphrase begins   is described by Frances Hill as a pushy, middle-aged, foul-
with the author's
name and ends   tempered outcast who smoked a pipe. If there were witches
with a page
reference in   in Salem village, she was sure to be one of them (36). When
parentheses.

Sarah begged for food and shelter for herself and her family,

she was often turned away by her neighbors. According to

Richard Weisman, Sarah often responded by "scolding and   No ellipsis is
                                                            needed when you
                                                            quote only short
cursing as a means of retaliation against unresponsive   phrases from a
                                                            source.
neighbors," and this behavior provided evidence for the

court and "generated a wealth of negative testimony" against

her (56). In addition to the testimony of the afflicted

girls, at least seven people who had witnessed Sarah's

disturbing behavior while begging testified against her in

court. Ironically, one of those people was her own husband.

Although he testified that he had never witnessed his wife

Piezzo 6

practicing witchcraft, he told the court that he feared Sarah

"'either was a witch or would be one very quickly'" (qtd. in

Weisman 56). He said that she treated him badly and described

her as "'an enemy to all good,'" apparently oblivious to the

pun on his name (qtd. in Weisman 56).

6   **Dorcas Good, Sarah's five-year-old daughter, also helped**

convict her mother. Dorcas was accused of witchcraft and ar-

rested, and in her terrified confession, she indicated that

her mother was indeed a witch. Sarah's young daughter spent

nine months chained up in a prison cell. Accused witches were

kept in chains because the Puritans believed the chains would

prevent their specters (the devil in human form) from flying

about doing evil deeds. Dorcas never recovered from the

trauma of her experience. In 1710 her father said, "'[S]he

hath ever since been very chargeable, having little or no

reason [with which] to govern herself'" (qtd. in Breslaw

171). By "chargeable" he meant that she was a great deal of

trouble and expense to him because she was unable to take

care of herself and had to be looked after for the rest of

her life. As a result of her experience in prison, she never

Single quotation marks inside double quotation marks show that words were in double quotation marks in the source.

Abbreviation "qtd." informs reader that quoted words are those of Sarah Good's husband and were not written by Weisman.

Topic sentence for paragraph 6.

Square brackets are used to change lowercase *s* in source to capital *S* because the first word in a quoted sentence must begin with a capital letter.

became a responsible member of her society. Dorcas's father

was in later years paid thirty pounds by Massachusetts as

reparation for the loss of his wife's life and his daughter's

sanity.

7   **By today's standards Sarah did not receive a fair trial.**

Topic sentence for paragraph 7.

Magistrates John Hathorne and Jonathan Corwin came to Salem

Village on March 1, 1692, to examine the accused witches.

Sarah Good was the first of the accused to be questioned by

Hathorne. It is obvious from the recorded testimony that

Full-sentence lead-in to quotation ends with a colon.

Hathorne believed Sarah was a witch:

Block quotation is indented one inch from the left margin. Double quotation marks in the source are retained in the quotation.

> "Sarah Good, what evil spirit have you
>
> familiarity with?"
>
> "None." Sarah answered defiantly.
>
> "Have you made no contract with the devil?"
>
> "No."
>
> "Why do you hurt these children?"
>
> "I do not hurt them. I scorn it."
>
> "Who do you employ then to do it?"
>
> "I employ nobody."
>
> "What creature do you employ then?"

Piezzo 8

"No creature, but I am falsely accused."

"Why did you go away muttering from Mr. Parris

his [sic] house?"

"I did not mutter but I thanked him for what he

gave my child [a reference to Sarah's daughter,

Dorcas Good]."

"Have you made no contract with the devil?"

"No." (qtd. in Hill 43)

Throughout her trial, Sarah remained defiant and never

confessed to being a witch.

8   **Highly questionable spectral evidence was also used to**

convict Sarah Good. Elizabeth Hubbard, at seventeen one of

the oldest of the "afflicted" girls, claimed that she saw

Sarah standing on the table in the home of Dr. Griggs "naked-

breasted and bare-legged and that if she had something to do

it with she would kill her" (Hill 66). Samuel Sibley, a Salem

inhabitant who was present at the time, "struck with his

staff where she pointed," and Elizabeth told those present

that he had struck Sarah's back (Hill 66). The next day in

court, the constable testified that Sarah's forearm was

Latin word [sic] explains that error appeared in source and was not Jessica's typing error.

Explanatory information is added to the quotation in square brackets.

Citation is placed after the period that ends the block quotation.

Topic sentence for paragraph 8.

If the author is not named in the sentence, the name must appear in the parenthetical citation.

Piezzo 9

bloody. This was considered evidence that Sarah Good's

specter had been struck by Sibley's staff at Dr. Griggs's

house--even though at the time Elizabeth, who was the only

person present who could actually see the supposed specter,

had told those present that the staff had hit Good's back. No

one apparently noticed this important discrepancy in relation

to the location of Sarah's supposed injury by Sibley, an

injury received while her physical body was not only chained

up, but locked in a prison cell.

9   **Some of the spectral evidence in Sarah Good's trial was**

clearly proved to be false. According to Katherine Sutcliffe,

a girl cried out during the trial that Sarah Good's specter

was stabbing her with a knife. Although part of a broken

knife was found in the girl's possession, a young man in the

courtroom stated that he had broken that same knife and had

thrown it away "in the presence of the afflicted girls." He

showed the constable the matching part of the broken knife as

proof that he was telling the truth (1). The girl, who had

clearly lied about her supposed injury at the hand of Good,

was simply told not to lie again, and the discovery that she

A dash is created by typing two hyphens with no spaces before, between, or after them.

Topic sentence for paragraph 9.

Summary of information from Sutcliffe begins with the author's name and ends with a page reference.

Piezzo 10

had lied to the court had no effect whatsoever on the outcome

Jessica gives her interpretation of the information she has summarized from Sutcliffe.

of the trial. The members of the Court of Oyer and Terminer

were clearly interested in finding evidence to convict Sarah,

not in making sure she got a fair trial. As one historian put

it, " '[T]here was no one in the country around against whom

Lowercase *t* in source changed to capital *T* in square brackets indicates that words were omitted before *there* in the source.

popular suspicion could have been more readily directed, or

in whose favor and defense less interest could be awakened' "

(qtd. in Sutcliffe 1).

10   **Sarah Good was sentenced to death by hanging on June 29,**

Topic sentence for paragraph 10.

1692. She was executed on July 19th. At her execution, she

showed no remorse, which only further convinced the people of

Salem Village that she was indeed a witch. On the way to

Gallows Hill, where the condemned witches were hanged, a min-

ister by the name of Nicholas Noyes attempted to get a con-

fession out of Sarah Good. She responded, " 'You are a liar.

Single quotation marks inside double quotation marks show that the words were in double quotation marks in the source.

I am no more a witch than you are a wizard, and if you take

away my life God will give you blood to drink' " (qtd. in

Sutcliffe 1). Ironically, Nicholas Noyes died some time later

from an internal hemorrhage. As Good had predicted, he died

with blood in his mouth (Sutcliffe 1).

Piezzo 11

11   What really happened in Salem Village, Massachusetts,

remains a mystery. The tragedy that occurred over three

hundred years ago intrigues historians to this day. Most of

the evidence that was presented against Sarah was hearsay,

which would never have been allowed in a courtroom today. It

seems clear, however, that no amount of evidence could have

proven that Sarah Good was innocent, for in the minds of the

townspeople and the judges, she had been guilty from the

start. **In the end, Sarah Good lost her life not because she**

had been practicing witchcraft, but because she was ill-

tempered, poor, and powerless.

Conclusion
Sentence: Jessica
explains why she
believes Good
was executed.

Piezzo 12

Works Consulted

Book in series.   Breslaw, Elaine G. <u>Tituba, Reluctant Witch of Salem: Devilish</u>

<u>Indians and Puritan Fantasies</u>. American Social

Experience Series 35. New York: New York UP, 1996.

Web site with no   "The Examination of Sarah Good, March 1, 1692." <u>Salem Trials</u>
author given.

<u>Home Page</u>. 11 Feb. 2000 <http://www.law.umkc.edu/faculty/

projects/ftrials/salem/ASA_GOOX.HTM>.

Scholarly journal   Gould, Philip. "New England Witch-Hunting and the Politics of
article.

Reason in the Early Republic." <u>New England Quarterly</u> 68

(1995): 58-82.

Book.   Hill, Frances. <u>A Delusion of Satan: The Full Story of the</u>

<u>Salem Witch Trials</u>. New York: Da Capo, 1997.

Web site with   Linder, Douglas. "An Account of Events in Salem." <u>Famous</u>
author given.

<u>Trials Home Page</u>. 1998. 30 Jan. 2000 <http://

www.law.umkc.edu/faculty/projects/ftrials/salem/

salem.htm>.

Article from an   Norton, Mary Beth. "Finding the Devil in the Details of the
online scholarly
journal.

Salem Witchcraft Trials." <u>Chronicle of Higher Education</u>

46.20 (2000): n. pag. 24 Jan. 2000 <http://chronicle.com/

weekly/v46/i20/20b00401.htm>.

Piezzo 13

"The Salem Witch Trials 1692: A Chronology of Events." <u>Salem

Home Page</u>. 27 Aug. 1997. Salem Office of Tourism and

Cultural Affairs. 10 Feb. 2000 <http://www.salemweb.com/

memorial/default.htm>.

Sutcliffe, Katherine. "Images from the Salem Witch Trials:

Sarah Good." <u>Salem Trials Home Page</u>. 12 Feb. 2000

<http://www.law.umkc.edu/faculty/projects/ftrials/salem/

SAL_BGOO.HTM>.

Watson, Bruce. "Salem's Dark Hour: Did the Devil Make Them Do

It?" <u>Smithsonian</u> Apr. 1992: 116-130. Full-text.

<u>InfoTrac: Expanded Academic ASAP</u>. Online. Gale

Group. 4 November 1999 <http://

web6.infotrac.galegroup.com>.

Weisman, Richard. <u>Witchcraft, Magic, and Religion in 17th

Century Massachusetts</u>. Amherst: U of Massachusetts P,

1984.

"Witchcraft in Salem Village." Danvers Archival Center of the

Peabody Institute Library of Danvers, MA, and Electronic

Text Center, U of Virginia. 5 Feb. 2000 <http://

etext.virginia.edu/salem/witchcraft/>.

Web site with no author given.

Web site with author given.

Full-text monthly magazine article from a subscription online database.

Book.

Web site with no author given.

CHAPTER 7

Sample Literary Analysis Research Paper

An Analysis of the Character Biff Loman in Death of a Salesman

By William E. Files

William Files was asked to analyze a character from a short story or play studied during the semester in his English 102 class. He chose to analyze Biff Loman from Arthur Miller's <u>Death of a Salesman</u>.

> **NOTE:** MLA DOES NOT REQUIRE YOU TO FORMAT YOUR THESIS, TOPIC SENTENCES, AND CONCLUSION SENTENCE IN BOLD. IN THIS TEXT, BOLD IS USED SIMPLY TO HELP YOU LOCATE THE CONTROLLING SENTENCES IN THE MODEL STUDENT ESSAYS.

William E. Files

Professor Schwartz

English 102: 9:30 MWF

7 December 1999

Outline

Title: An Analysis of the Character Biff Loman in <u>Death of a</u>

<u>Salesman</u>

Audience: General Audience

Word Count: 1,241

Thesis: Biff achieves what eludes every other character in

this story--a change in identity and a casting off of his

father's old image of him.

Topic Sentence 1: Biff's first life-changing experience

drastically alters his opinion of his father.

Topic Sentence 2: In the present and back at home, Biff tells

his father that he is going to see Bill Oliver, for whom he

claims to have once worked as a salesman, to ask for a loan

to start a business of his own selling sporting goods.

Topic Sentence 3: When Biff realizes what a waste his life

has been, he feels the need to confront his father.

Topic Sentence 4: His father's death changes Biff, allowing him to become fully himself with no one else's imposing sense of the world weighing him down.

Conclusion Sentence: Having at last escaped the tenacious grasp of his father's dreams and illusions, Biff Loman can finally be his own person and live out his own dreams and destiny, unburdened with his father's false guidance.

Honor Pledge: Except as documented on my works-cited page, I received no help on this essay other than a discussion with my brother Michael about the play and its characters and editing assistance from Professor Schwartz.

Use one-inch top,
bottom, left, and
right margins.

Your name and
page number
should be a
header appearing
one-half inch
from the top
of the page.

Type your name,
your professor's
name, class name
and time, and
paper due date
at the top left
margin of your
paper.

William E. Files

Professor Schwartz

English 102: 9:30 MWF

7 December 1999

An Analysis of the Character Biff Loman

in <u>Death of a Salesman</u>

Centered title
explains exactly
what will be
discussed in the
paper.

Author, genre,
and title of work
should be identi-
fied in the first
sentence of a
literary analysis
essay.

1   Arthur Miller's play <u>Death of a Salesman</u> tells the story

of Willy Loman, a salesman living in Brooklyn, New York, and

his family. At the heart of the play is the strained rela-

tionship between Willy and his eldest son, Biff. In Willy's

Analyze literary
works in the
present tense.

world, the qualities that will get a man ahead in life are

his good looks and his charm, so he tells his boys, "[T]he

No ellipsis is
needed to show
omission of words
at beginning of
quoted sentence
because lower-
case *t* in source
is changed in
square brackets
to capital *T*.

man who makes an appearance in the business world, the man

who creates personal interest, is the man who gets ahead. Be

liked and you will never want" (Miller 1489). He is so

If the author is
not named in the
lead-in to the
quotation, the
name must be
placed in the
parenthetical
citation.

obsessed with Biff's good looks and masculine charm that he

builds him up to be a successful businessman and expects

nothing short of that. Biff has always been imbued with the

values of his father and the goal of monetary success, but

after a series of illuminating, though traumatic events, he

Files 2

finally begins to develop his own identity and values

separate from his father's. **In the end, Biff achieves what**

eludes every other character in this story--a change in

identity and a casting off of his father's old image of him.

2   **Biff's first life-changing experience drastically alters**

his opinion of his father. Prior to his graduation from high

school, Biff makes plans to attend the University of Virginia

on a full football scholarship. His graduation is imperiled,

however, when he fails his senior math course. Biff goes to

Boston to ask his father to talk to the math teacher for him.

Jeffrey Helterman suggests that Biff, following his father's

example, believes that having his father convince his math

teacher to pass him would be easier than taking the class

again during the summer and is therefore the correct

choice (93). When Biff gets to Willy's hotel room, he finds

his father with a scantily clad woman and thus discovers

Willy's infidelity. This is a real turning point for Biff,

and he begins to view his father as a liar, a fake, and a

phony. Jeffrey Helterman points out that

        Willy never stops selling himself, and selling

        means improving the product--making it sound

Sidebar annotations:

Thesis statement. The purpose of this essay is to present evidence to convince the reader that this thesis statement is true.

Topic sentence for paragraph 2.

Paraphrase of Helterman's analysis begins with the critic's name and ends with the page in a parenthetical citation, which is placed before the period ending the sentence.

A quotation introduction ending in "that" needs no punctuation.

A dash is created by typing two hyphens with no spaces before, between, or after them.

Files 3

Long block
quotation is
indented one
inch from the
left margin. No
quotation marks
are used because
the blocking
identifies the
material as a
quote.

> better than it is. His report of his selling
>
> trips, even on his best days, are always exaggera-
>
> tions, the step to outright lies is only a small
>
> one, and Hap inherits this trait from his father.
>
> Biff goes along with Willy's petty cheating until
>
> he discovers that Willy has cheated even on his
>
> own wife. (93)

From this point forward Biff looks at his father through

disillusioned eyes and starts to see that his father's way

is skewed. Biff's burning of his tennis shoes symbolizes his

throwing away his plans to go to the University of Virginia,

and thereby dashing Willy's hopes for his son to become a

successful businessman.

3   **In the present and back at home, Biff tells his father**   Topic sentence for
paragraph 3.

that he is going to see Bill Oliver, for whom he claims to

have once worked as a salesman, to ask for a loan to start a

sporting goods business. Biff knows he does not have any

interest or real skill in the business world, yet he does

Paraphrase of
Harshbarger's
analysis begins
with the critic's
name and ends
with the page
citation.   this to please his father. As Karl Harshbarger points out,

Biff deludes himself into believing that he can succeed in a

sports equipment business by getting a loan from Bill Oliver.

Files 4

He lies to himself to build up his confidence that he can

create this new business career for himself, even though the

thought of a nine-to-five job in the business world fills

him with horror (44). When his attempted meeting with Oliver

turns out to be a complete failure, it finally dawns on Biff

what a phony and a loser he is and "what a ridiculous lie my

whole life has been!" (Miller 1527). Harshbarger explains:

An exclamation point or question mark ending quoted material is placed inside closing quotation marks and before the parenthetical citation.

> Oliver's rejection, in fact, has a stunning effect
>
> on Biff. He can tell Happy, "I'm all numb, I
>
> swear," and he talks about what happened in
>
> Oliver's office "with great tension and wonder"
>
> [emphasis Harshbarger's]. After having evaluated
>
> Biff's past we can see that this event repeats a
>
> chronic problem for Biff: the surfacing of the
>
> knowledge that he is not a man, that he is a
>
> failure. (44)

Double quotation marks from the original source are retained in a block quotation.

Bracketed material explains that underlining appeared in the source and was not done by William.

4   **When Biff realizes what a waste his life has been, he**

feels the need to confront his father. After meeting Happy

at a restaurant, Biff tries to explain to him that the Loman

family is caught in a web of deceit, but Happy, like his

Topic sentence for paragraph 4.

Files 5

father, refuses to hear what Biff is trying to tell him. When

Willy shows up, he tells the boys he has been fired. Biff

wastes no time trying to tell his father about his experience

with Oliver, but Willy won't listen, so Biff gives up and

instead tells Willy what he wants to hear--that he has

another appointment with Oliver the next day. A now more

realistic Biff realizes, however, that having stolen a gold

pen from Oliver's desk, he cannot go back to see Oliver

again. At this point, Willy starts having flashbacks to the

Boston incident and goes to the bathroom to escape from Biff

and the guilt he feels about ruining his beloved son's life.

The boys leave their father alone in the restaurant, setting

the stage for the final confrontation of the play.

5   Later that night, Biff comes home and explains to Willy

that it would be best for them to never see each other again.

Biff cannot, until the final moments of his time with Willy,

articulate his contempt for Willy's life of illusions. He

tries once again to explain that he is "not a leader of men,"

that he is in fact "a dime a dozen" (Miller 1543). Willy

denies this self-assessment and tells Biff once again how

William explains the changes he finds in Biff's behavior as he analyzes this scene.

No ellipses are needed when you quote short phrases from the source.

great he can be. Willy refuses to see the truth, and this

frustrates Biff to the point that he breaks down and sobs,

asking Willy to forget him. However, as Neil Carson points

out, "Willy has too much emotional capital tied up in his

dreams of Biff's magnificence, and he prefers to sacrifice

his life rather than his illusion" (56). He has in mind one

last business deal: to cash in on his twenty-thousand-dollar

life insurance policy by killing himself. This will set Biff

up financially, transferring his unfulfilled dream of

business success onto his son. Willy drives out into the

night and crashes his car, killing himself. At the funeral,

however, Biff assures his brother Happy, "I know who I am

[. . .]" (Miller 1546). **His father's death has changed Biff,**

allowing him to become fully himself with no one else's

imposing sense of the world weighing him down.

6   The traumatic discovery of his father's infidelity in

Boston, the eye-opening meeting with Bill Oliver, and the

reality of his father's suicide take Biff to a new awareness.

These events change his view of himself, his father, and the

world. Traumatic events in life often give people new insight

---

Short quotation begins with the critic's name in lead-in and ends with the page reference, which is placed before the period that ends the sentence.

Bracketed ellipsis (three spaced periods) indicates that one or more words were omitted at the end of the quotation.

Topic sentence for paragraph 5.

Files 7

which helps them become more aware of themselves and of their

surroundings. **Having at last escaped the tenacious grasp of**

his father's dreams and illusions, Biff Loman can finally be

his own person and live out his own dreams and destiny,

unburdened with his father's false guidance.

Conclusion
sentence reminds
reader of the main
point of the essay.

Works Cited

Book in a series.

Carson, Neil. Arthur Miller. Grove Press Modern Dramatists.

New York: Grove, 1982.

Book.

Harshbarger, Karl. The Burning Jungle: An Analysis of Arthur

Miller's Death of a Salesman. Washington: UP of America,

1977.

Article from a
literary reference
book.

Helterman, Jeffrey. "Arthur Miller." Twentieth-Century

American Dramatists. Part 2. Ed. John MacNicholas. Vol.

7 of Dictionary of Literary Biography. Detroit: Gale,

1981. 86-111.

Miller play from a
literary anthology.

Miller Arthur. Death of a Salesman. Literature: An

Introduction to Fiction, Poetry, and Drama. Ed. X. J.

Kennedy and Dana Gioia. 6th ed. New York: Harper, 1995.

1476-1547.

Files 9

Additional Works Consulted

Centola, Steven. "Family Values in <u>Death of a Salesman</u>." <u>CLA</u>   Scholarly journal article.

<u>Journal</u> 37 (1993): 29-41.

Dudar, Helen. "A Modern Tragedy's Road to Maturity." <u>New York</u>   Newspaper article.

<u>Times</u> 25 March 1984, late ed., sec. 2: 1+.

Hogan, Robert. "Arthur Miller." <u>American Writers: A</u>   Article from a literary reference book.

<u>Collection of Literary Biographies</u>. Ed. Leonard Unger.

Vol. 3. New York: Scribner's, 1974. 145-69.

Lawrence, Stephen A. "The Right Dream in Miller's <u>Death of a</u>   Scholarly journal article.

<u>Salesman</u>." <u>College English</u> 25 (1964): 547-49.

"Miller, Arthur." <u>Encyclopedia Americana</u>. 1994 ed.   Article from a general encyclopedia.

Scholarly journal article reprinted in an essay collection.   Parker, Brian. "Point of View in Arthur Miller's <u>Death of a</u>

<u>Salesman</u>." <u>University of Toronto Quarterly</u> 35 (1996):

144-57. Rpt. in <u>Arthur Miller: A Collection of Critical</u>

<u>Essays</u>. Ed. Robert W. Corrigan. Englewood Cliffs, NJ:

Prentice, 1969. 95-109.

Phelps, H. C. "Miller's <u>Death of a Salesman</u>." <u>The Explicator</u>   Scholarly journal article.

53 (1994): 239-40.

CHAPTER 8

Preparing Your Bibliography

General Guidelines for Preparing Your Bibliography

The word **bibliography** literally means a list of books used to prepare a paper. Because modern researchers typically use many nonprint as well as printed sources to prepare research papers, the titles **Works Cited** and **Works Consulted** are more appropriate. In this discussion, the general term **bibliography** is used to refer to either a works-cited or a works-consulted list.

The bibliography is titled **Works Cited** if it lists only the sources from which you quoted, paraphrased, or summarized in the paper.

It is titled **Works Consulted** if it lists not only the sources from which you quoted, paraphrased, or summarized but also other sources that you read but from which you did not cite materials.

If you want to inform your instructor about all the works you used in preparing the paper whether or not you cited from them, prepare a works-consulted list and include all the works that provided useful information. Do not include sources you used to find the materials you actually read. For example, if you used the <u>New York Times Index</u> to find a useful article in the <u>New York Times</u>, cite the article, not the index you used to find the article. (See works-consulted lists on pages 46–47 and 170–71.)

A third option is to give both a works-cited list containing the sources from which you cited material and a second list entitled **Additional Works Consulted** in which you list sources you read but from which you did not take cited information. (See William Files's works-cited/additional works–consulted lists on pages 58–59.)

Works are listed alphabetically by the author's last name or, if no author is given, by the first significant word of the title excluding *A, An,* and *The.*

The first line of each entry should be typed flush with the left margin. If the entry contains more than one line, indent each line after the first line one-half inch (on a computer) or five spaces (on a typewriter) from the left margin. This is called a hanging indent.

Double-space the entire works-cited list.

The works-cited list is the last page of your paper and should be numbered as part of your text. If you use an endnote page, number it as part of your text, and place it before the works-cited list.

Creating a Hanging Indent in Microsoft Word

To create a hanging indent, first highlight or select the material you want to appear in hanging indent format. Then go to the "Format" menu at the top of your screen. Go to "Paragraph." Under "Indentation," go to "Special." Highlight "Hanging." Click on "OK." Your first line should now be flush with the left margin of your text and all subsequent lines in the same entry should be indented one-half inch from the left margin.

Removing a Hanging Indent in Microsoft Word

To remove a hanging indent, highlight or select the material you want not to appear in hanging indent format. Then go to the "Format" menu at the top of your screen. Go to "Paragraph." Under "Indentation," go to "Special." Highlight "(none)." Click on "OK."

Center the title **Works Cited** or **Works Consulted** (not underlined and not in quotation marks; not in bold or italics) one inch from the top of the page. Double-space between the title and the first entry in your list.

If publication information does not appear on the title page or copyright page (on the back of the title page), look for it in the card catalog, online catalog, or other sources and give the information in square brackets to show that the information is known, but was not given in your source: New York: Harper, [1992].

If publication information is unavailable (does not exist), use the following abbreviations so your reader will know that you would have given the information if it had been available. Note that MLA recommends leaving no spaces in the abbreviations *n.p.* and *n.d.*

- **No place of publication given:** N.p.: Houghton, 1994.
- **No publisher given:** Boston: n.p., 1994.
- **No date of publication given:** Boston: Houghton, n.d.
- **No pages given for a book entry:** Boston: Houghton, 1994. N. pag.
- **No pages given for a journal entry:** College English 52 (1992): n. pag.

Leave one space after commas, semicolons, and colons and two spaces after periods, question marks, and exclamation points. One space after all marks is standard to save space in material prepared for publication, however.

To create a dash, type two hyphens with no space before, between, or after the hyphens:

```
He was--let there be no mistake about it--the guilty person.
```

Shortening Numbers

When citing inclusive page numbers in a bibliographic entry, give the complete numbers for any number between one and ninety-nine: 4–5; 12–17; 22–24; 78–93.

You may shorten numbers over ninety-nine unless the second number would be unclear. Numbers such as these are clear: 107–09; 245–47; 1710–12; 1002–09; 1408–578. Shortening would be unclear for numbers such as these, so give the complete numbers: 287–305; 956–1023; 87–127.

Preparing an Annotated Bibliography

If your professor asks you to prepare an annotated bibliography, alphabetize your citations by author or by the first significant word of the title (excluding *A*, *An*, and *The*) if no author is known. Follow each citation with a brief summary of the contents of the source. Here is a sample entry from an annotated bibliography:

```
Norton, Mary Beth. "Finding the Devil in the Details of the

     Salem Witchcraft Trials." Chronicle of Higher Education

     46.20 (2000): n. pag. 5 Jan. 2000 <http://chronicle.com/

     weekly/v46/i20/20b00401.htm>.


Mary Beth Norton, a professor of history at Cornell University,

notes that previous accusations of witchcraft in the New En-

gland area targeted what she terms a few and never more than a

dozen of what she calls "'the usual suspects'"--people who had

long been suspected of practicing witchcraft by their neigh-

bors. However, in Salem Village and the surrounding towns of

Essex County, Massachusetts, hundreds of people were accused,

and although some of those accused were "'the usual suspects,'"
```

many had never been suspected of any witch-like behavior before. She believes the hysteria may be explained by fear of the Indian attacks that were occurring at the time. In fact, there was an attack only twenty miles from Salem Village while the trials were being held. Many believed that the devil and his minions were aiding the Indians; therefore, anyone consorting with the devil at that particular historical moment would have been seen as a threat to the survival of the village.

Citing Titles Correctly in a Works-Cited List

Capitalize the first and last words of the title and subtitle and all other words with the exception of

- articles (*a, an, the*),
- prepositions (*in, on, to, under, between, over, through, etc.*),
- the seven coordinating conjunctions (FANBOYS: *for, and, nor, but, or, yet, so*), and
- the word *to* used in infinitives (*to* see, *to* run, *to* jump, etc.).

> FOLLOW THE STANDARD CAPITALIZATION RULES DESCRIBED HERE FOR ALL TITLES AND SUBTITLES EVEN THOUGH THOSE RULES MAY NOT HAVE BEEN FOLLOWED ON THE TITLE PAGE OF THE BOOK OR ARTICLE YOU ARE CITING.

Underline the titles of works that were published as or that exist as separate entities: books, plays, book-length poems, scholarly journals, popular magazines, newspapers, pamphlets, films, television series, records, compact discs, audiocassettes, paintings, sculpted works, ships, planes, and so on.

Use double quotation marks around the title of a work too short to be published as a separate entity: for example, a short story; an essay; a short poem; a chapter in a book; a lecture; an article in a scholarly journal, popular magazine, newspaper, dictionary, reference book, or encyclopedia; one episode of a television series; one song on a record, compact disc, or audiocassette.

If a title or quotation that should be placed in quotation marks appears within the title of an article or essay you are citing, use single quotation marks around the title of the short story, poem, essay, or quotation, and use double quotation marks around the title of the article or essay.

```
"An Analysis of the Symbolism in Faulkner's 'A Rose for

Emily.' "
```

If an essay or journal article title contains the title of a work that should be underlined (novel, play, work of art, etc.), use double quotation marks around the essay title and underline the secondary title.

```
"Female Characters in Faulkner's The Sound and the Fury."
```

If a book title contains the title of another work that should also be underlined, underline the main title, but not the secondary title.

```
A Reader's Guide to Moby Dick.
```

CHAPTER 9

Citing Books and Parts of Books

Citing Books

A Book with One Author

Richardson, William C. <u>Emily Dickinson: Her Life and Poetry</u>.

    3rd ed. New York: Random, 1994.

1. Give the author's name exactly as it appears on the title page, inverted for alphabetizing. Do not omit initials or shorten first or middle names to initials.
2. You may use initials if they appear on the title page: Eliot, T. S. You may clarify initials in square brackets if you think the clarification would be useful to your reader: Eliot, T[homas] S[tearns].
3. Place an essential suffix after the name: Russell, John E., Jr. or Smith, Wilson R., IV.
4. Omit degrees or other titles (*PhD, Sister, Saint, Sir, Lady*).
5. If the author uses a pen name, you may give the author's real name in square brackets after the pseudonym: Twain, Mark [Samuel Langhorne Clemens].
6. Give both the title and the subtitle of a book. Use a colon between the title and subtitle. If there is a question mark, exclamation point, or dash after the main title, omit the colon.
7. Type a continuous line under the title and subtitle, but do not underline the period that follows the title: <u>Sylvia Plath: A Critical Study</u>.
8. If the title ends with a question mark or exclamation point, omit the usual end period and underline the final punctuation mark: <u>Absalom! Absalom!</u>
9. Use underlining rather than italics for book titles because italics are not as easily noticed by your reader as underlining.
10. Give the first city of publication listed on the title page.
11. Give the state, province for Canadian cities, or country only if the city is not well known or could be confused with another city: for example, Upper Saddle River, NJ; Charleston, SC; Charleston, WV; Rome, GA; Rome, NY; Rome, It.; Cambridge, MA; Cambridge, Eng.
12. You may omit the state if the publisher's name identifies it: Baton Rouge: Louisiana State UP, 1998.

13. If you give the state, use the standard postal abbreviation without periods. Use MLA recommended abbreviations for countries (*Eng.* for *England*, *It.* for *Italy*) and provinces of Canada (*ON* for *Ontario*, *PQ* for *Quebec*). (See abbreviations for states, Canadian provinces, and countries in chapter 22.)

14. Shorten the publisher's name to one significant word: Houghton Mifflin, Co. becomes Houghton; W. W. Norton and Co., Inc. becomes Norton; McGraw-Hill, Inc. becomes McGraw, and so on. Give the full name of a university press, however, using the abbreviations *U* for *University* and *P* for *Press:* U of Chicago P; Yale UP; Oxford UP. (See chapter 23 for more information on shortening the names of publishers.)

15. You need not give a publisher for a book published before 1900: London, 1878.

16. Give the most recent publication date listed on the title page or copyright page (the back of the title page). If no date of publication is given, give the most recent copyright date listed. If no date of publication or copyright can be found, use *n.d.* in place of the date.

Two or More Books by the Same Author

Smith, Charles R. <u>Robert Frost's Poetry</u>. 2nd ed. New York: Random, 1994.

---. <u>Symbolism in Robert Frost's Poetry</u>. New York: Harper, 1995.

---, ed. <u>The Writing Style of Robert Frost: A Collection of Critical Essays</u>. Boston: Houghton, 1995.

---, trans. <u>A Young Reader's Guide to the Poetry of Robert Frost</u>. By John T. Collins. Englewood Cliffs, NJ: Prentice, 1997.

1. The three hyphens used in place of the author's name mean that the book was written by the same author you cited in the previous entry, not that no author is known. (If no author is known, begin the entry with the title.)

2. Type a comma, one space, and the appropriate abbreviation after the three hyphens to indicate that the person is an editor (ed.), translator (trans.), or compiler (comp.) rather than an author.

3. List two or more books by the same person alphabetically by the first significant word of the title excluding *A, An,* and *The.*

A Book with an Editor instead of an Author

```
Yeazell, Ruth Bernard, ed. Henry James: A Collection of Criti-
    cal Essays. New Century Views. Englewood Cliffs, NJ: Pren-
    tice, 1994.
```

A Book with an Author and an Editor

```
Whitman, Walt. Complete Poetry and Selected Prose. Ed. James E.
    Miller, Jr. Riverside Edition. Boston: Houghton, 1959.

Miller, James E., Jr., ed. Complete Poetry and Selected Prose.
    By Walt Whitman. Riverside Edition. Boston: Houghton,
    1959.
```

If you are citing material written by the author, begin your entry with the author's name and place the editor's name after the title preceded by the abbreviation *Ed.* (*Edited by*). However, if you are primarily citing material written by the editor, such as the introduction, explanatory materials, or notes, give the editor's name first, followed by the abbreviation *ed.* (*editor*) or *eds.* (*editors*) for more than one editor. After the title type *By,* and give the author's name.

A Book with Two Authors

```
Harrison, Samuel W., and Benjamin R. Wright. Movies in the
    Twentieth Century. Cambridge, MA: Harvard UP, 1994.
```

1. Give the authors' names in the same order as they appear on the title page.
2. If both authors have the same last name, give both names in full.
3. Invert only the name of the first author.

A Book with Three Authors

```
Peabody, Charles T., Robert N. James, Jr., and Sylvia W.
    Samuels. Ernest Hemingway: The Early Years. Rev. ed. New
    York: St. Martin's, 1993.
```

1. Give all three names in the same order as the names appear on the title page.
2. Invert only the name of the first author.

A Book with Four or More Authors

Hodges, John C., et al. <u>Hodges' Harbrace Handbook</u>. 14th ed.

    Fort Worth: Harcourt, 2001.

1. Give the name of the first author listed, and then type *et al.*, which means "and others." Note that *al.* is an abbreviation of the Latin word *alii*; therefore, it is always followed by a period.
2. If you prefer, you may give the names of all the authors in the order that they are given on the title page. Invert only the name of the first author.

An Edition Other Than the First

Sydney, Beatrice E. <u>A Study of James Joyce</u>. 2nd ed. Boston:

    Little, 1992.

1. If the book is not a first edition, give the edition number specified on the title page—*2nd ed.; 3rd ed.; 4th ed.; Rev. ed.* (for *Revised edition*); *Abr. ed.* (for *Abridged edition*)—after the title. Use MLA recommended abbreviations for edition numbers. (See chapter 22 for a list of MLA-recommended abbreviations for editions.)
2. If an editor's, translator's, or compiler's name appears after the title, give the edition number after the editor's, translator's, or compiler's name.

A Book in a Series

Wilson, C. Philip, Charles C. Hogan, and Ira L. Mintz, eds.

    <u>Fear of Being Fat: The Treatment of Anorexia Nervosa and</u>

    <u>Bulimia</u>. Classical Psychoanalysis and Its Applications.

    New York: Aronson, 1983.

1. If the book you are citing is part of a series of books, the series name and sometimes a series number will be given above the title of the book or on the page opposite the title page (called the half-title page).
2. Give the name of the series (not underlined and not in quotation marks) before the publication information and followed by a period.

3. If a series number is given, type it immediately after the series name, inside the period: Gale Author Series 2.

A Publisher's Imprint

Meyer, Michael. <u>Thinking and Writing about Literature</u>. Boston:

    Bedford-St. Martin's, 1995.

Sometimes publishers group some of their books under special names called publishers' imprints. If an imprint name appears on the title page along with the publisher's name, type the imprint name, a hyphen, and then type the publisher's name (Bedford-St. Martin's; Vintage-Random; Anchor-Doubleday; Longman-Addison).

A Multivolume Work

Smithfield, Raymond C. <u>The Novels of Thomas Hardy</u>. 4 vols.

    Boston: Little, 1988-93.

1. After the title, give the editor's name if there is one, the edition number if the book is not a first edition, and the total number of volumes in the work.
2. If you cite material from several volumes of a multivolume work, identify the volume you used in your parenthetical citation: (Smithfield 2: 345).
3. Give the inclusive dates if the volumes were published over a period of years: 1955–62.
4. If the work is still in progress, give the number of volumes currently available (2 vols. to date). Give the date the first volume was published, type a hyphen, one space, and a period (1996– .).

One Volume of a Multivolume Work

Dixon, Murphey R. <u>George Eliot: A Biography</u>. 2nd ed. Vol. 2.

    Oxford, Eng.: Oxford UP, 1992. 4 vols.

1. If you used only one volume, give the volume number after the title, editor, and edition number if there is one.
2. Give publication information only for the volume you used.
3. If you wish, you can give the total number of volumes after the publication information.

A Translation

Sophocles. <u>Oedipus the King</u>. Trans. Francis Storr. Ed. T. E.

Page and W. H. D. Rouse. London: Heinemann, 1912.

Citing Parts of Books

A Chapter in a Book

Crews, Frederick. "Psychological Romance." <u>The Sins of the Fa-</u>

<u>thers: Hawthorne's Psychological Themes</u>. New York: Oxford

UP, 1966. 3-26.

An Introduction, Preface, Foreword, or Afterword

Johnson, Thomas H. Introduction. <u>The Complete Poems of Emily</u>

<u>Dickinson</u>. Ed. Johnson. Boston: Little, 1960. v-xi.

Miller, James E., Jr. Introduction. <u>Complete Poetry and Se-</u>

<u>lected Prose</u>. By Walt Whitman. Ed. Miller. Riverside Edi-

tion. Boston: Houghton, 1959. xix-liii.

Graff, Gerald. Preface. <u>Beyond the Culture Wars: How Teaching</u>

<u>the Conflicts Can Revitalize American Education</u>. By Graff.

New York: Norton, 1992. vii-x.

Frost, Robert. "The Figure a Poem Makes." Preface. <u>Collected</u>

<u>Poems</u>. By Frost. New York: Holt, 1939. v-ix.

1. Give the author of the introduction, preface, foreward, or afterword.
2. Capitalize, but do not underline or use quotation marks around the appropriate title: *Introduction, Preface, Foreword,* or *Afterword.*
3. If the introduction, preface, foreword, or afterword has a title, give it in double quotation marks. Then give the name of the part (not underlined or in quotation marks) followed by the title of the book (underlined).
4. Type the word *By* after the title and give the full name of the author of the book if different from the writer of the introduction, preface, foreword, or afterword and not given in the title of the book.
5. If the author of the book also wrote the introduction, preface, foreword, or afterword, type the word *By* after the title of the book and give only the author's last name.

6. Type *Ed.* (which means *Edited by*) and give the name of the editor (if there is one) after the name of the author.
7. If the editor of the book also wrote the introduction, preface, foreword, or afterword, type the word *By* after the title of the book and give only the editor's last name.

Citing Anthologies and Works in Anthologies

An Edited Anthology

McMichael, George, ed. <u>Concise Anthology of American Litera-</u>

<u>ture</u>. 4th ed. Upper Saddle River, NJ: Prentice, 1998.

A Short Story, Poem, or Essay in an Anthology

Crane, Stephen. "The Open Boat." <u>Literature: An Introduction to</u>

<u>Fiction, Poetry, and Drama</u>. Ed. X. J. Kennedy and Dana

Gioia. 7th ed. New York: Longman-Addison, 1999. 177-95.

1. Type quotation marks around the title of the short story, poem, or essay. Underline the title of the anthology.
2. At the end of the entry, give the first page and the last page of the story, poem, or essay, separated with a hyphen.

A Play in an Anthology

Williams, Tennessee. <u>The Glass Menagerie</u>. <u>Literature: An Introduc-</u>

<u>tion to Fiction, Poetry, and Drama</u>. Ed. X. J. Kennedy and

Dana Gioia. 7th ed. New York: Longman-Addison, 1999. 1710-61.

1. Underline the title of the play and of the anthology in which it is printed.
2. At the end of the entry, give the first page of the play, type a hyphen, and give the last page of the play.

A Novel in an Anthology

Twain, Mark [Samuel Langhorne Clemens]. <u>The Adventures of Huck-</u>

<u>leberry Finn</u>. <u>Concise Anthology of American Literature</u>.

Ed. George McMichael. 3rd ed. Upper Saddle River, NJ:

Prentice, 1998. 1235-1419.

1. Underline the title of the novel and of the anthology in which it appears.
2. At the end of the entry, give the first page of the novel, type a hyphen, and give the last page of the novel.
3. If the author uses a pen name, you may give the author's real name in square brackets after the pseudonym.

Cross-Referencing Works from an Anthology

When you are citing several literary works from the same anthology, avoid unnecessary repetition in your works-cited list by cross-referencing. For example, suppose you quote lines from an essay, a short story, a poem, a play, and a novel all collected in the same anthology. Give a complete bibliographical citation for the anthology, then cross-reference each of the literary works you used from the anthology by following the guidelines listed here. List the cross-referenced citations in alphabetical order by last name of the author or editor (or by the title if no author/editor is known).

A Poem

Stevens, Wallace. "Sunday Morning." McMichael 1789-92.

An Essay

Emerson, Ralph Waldo. "Self-Reliance." McMichael 676-93.

A Short Story

Hemingway, Ernest. "The Short Happy Life of Francis Macomber."
     McMichael 1888-1909.

An Entire Anthology

McMichael, George, ed. Concise Anthology of American Litera-
     ture. 4th ed. Upper Saddle River, NJ: Prentice, 1998.

A Play

Miller, Arthur. Death of a Salesman. McMichael 1996-2060.

A Novel

Twain, Mark. The Adventures of Huckleberry Finn. McMichael
     1235-1419.

1. Give the author(s) of the essay, short story, poem, play, or novel.

2. Give the title of an essay, short poem, or short story in double quotation marks followed by a period inside the final quotation mark.

3. Underline the title of a book-length poem, play, or novel, but do not underline the period that follows the title.

4. If one particular literary work (but not the contents of the entire anthology) was translated from a foreign language into English, type *Trans.* (which means *translated by*) after the title of the work, and give the name of the translator followed by a period (Trans. James T. Woods.).

5. Give the last name of the editor of the anthology and the inclusive pages of the essay, short story, poem, play, or novel followed by a period. Do not type a period or comma between the name of the editor(s) of the anthology and the page numbers of the work. A period would be needed if you used the Latin phrase *et alii* (which means *and others* in Latin) after the name of the editor because *al.* is always abbreviated (Roberts et al. 24–46.).

6. If you are citing two or more works by the editor of this anthology, type a comma after the editor's name and give the full or a shortened form of the title after the editor's name and before the inclusive page numbers of the work.

Citing Essays

An Essay Written for a Collection of Essays

```
Martin, Samuel A. "Willy Loman: A Modern Tragic Hero." Arthur

    Miller: A Collection of Essays. Ed. Glenn T. Richardson.

    Boston: Houghton, 1992. 72-84.
```

Cross-Referencing Essays from a Collection of Essays

When you are citing several essays from the same essay collection, avoid unnecessary repetition in your works-cited list by cross-referencing. For example, suppose you cite information from three scholarly essays analyzing twentieth-century American poetry. Give a complete bibliographical citation for the entire collection; then cross-reference each of the essays you used by following the guidelines given here. List the cross-referenced citations in alphabetical order by the last name of the author or editor (or by the title if no author/editor is known).

Daniels, Kate. "The Demise of the 'Delicate Prisons': The

Woman's Movement in Twentieth-Century American Poetry."

Myers and Wojahn 224-53.

Hirsch, Edward. "Helmet of Fire: American Poetry in the 1920s."

Myers and Wojahn 54-83.

Myers, Jack, and David Wojahn, eds. <u>A Profile of Twentieth-

Century American Poetry</u>. Carbondale: Southern Illinois

UP, 1991.

Ullman, Leslie. "American Poetry in the 1960s." Myers and

Wojahn 190-223.

1. Give the author(s) of the essay.
2. Give the title of the essay in double quotation marks with a period inside the final quotation mark. If there is a title that should also be in quotation marks within the essay title, place the secondary title in single quotation marks.
3. If one particular essay (but not the entire collection) was translated from a foreign language into English, type *Trans.* (which means *translated by*) after the title of the essay, and give the name of the translator (Trans. Robert K. Moore.).
4. Give the last name(s) of the editor(s) of the essay collection and the inclusive pages of the essay followed by a period.
5. If you are citing two or more works by the editor(s) of this collection, type a comma after the name(s) of the editor(s) and give the full or a shortened form of the title after the name(s) of the editor(s) and before the inclusive page numbers for the essay (Myers and Wojahn, <u>Profile</u> 190–223. Myers and Wojahn, <u>Study</u> 205–10.).

Citing Reprinted Essays, Articles, and Excerpts

A Scholarly Journal Article Reprinted in an Essay Collection

Seltzer, Mark. "Surveillance in <u>The Princess Casamassima</u>."

<u>Nineteenth-Century Fiction</u> 35 (1981): 506-34. Rpt. in

<u>Henry James: A Collection of Critical Essays</u>. Ed. Ruth

Bernard Yeazell. Englewood Cliffs, NJ: Prentice, 1994.

98-117.

1. Tell your reader where and when the article was first printed. The original publication information is usually given at the bottom of the first page of the article.
2. Then type *Rpt. in* ("reprinted in") and give full publication information on the essay collection you actually used.

An Excerpt from a Book Reprinted in an Essay Collection

Porter, Carolyn. "Gender and Value in <u>The American</u>." <u>New Essays</u>

<u>on</u> The American. Ed. Martha Banta. Cambridge: Cambridge

UP, 1987. 99-125. Rpt. in <u>Henry James: A Collection of</u>

<u>Critical Essays</u>. Ed. Ruth Bernard Yeazell. Englewood

Cliffs, NJ: Prentice, 1994. 39-59.

1. Tell your reader where and when the material was first printed. The original publication information is usually given at the bottom of the first page of the article.
2. Then type *Rpt. in* ("reprinted in") and give full publication information on the essay collection you actually used.

A Scholarly Journal Article Reprinted in a Critical Edition

Abel, Darrel. "Hawthorne's Hester." <u>College English</u> 13 (1952):

303-09. Rpt. in <u>The Scarlet Letter: An Authoritative Text,</u>

<u>Essays in Criticism and Scholarship</u>. By Nathaniel Haw-

thorne. Ed. Seymour Gross et al. 3rd ed. Norton Critical

Edition. New York: Norton, 1988. 300-08.

An Excerpt from a Book Reprinted in a Critical Edition

Male, Roy R. "[Transformations: Hester and Arthur.]" <u>Haw-</u>

<u>thorne's Tragic Vision</u>. Austin: U of Texas P, 1957. 102-17.

Rpt. in <u>The Scarlet Letter: An Authoritative Text, Essays</u>

<u>in Criticism and Scholarship</u>. By Nathaniel Haw-

thorne. Ed. Seymour Gross et al. 3rd ed. Norton Critical

Edition. New York: Norton, 1988. 325-35.

1. Tell your reader where and when the material was first printed. The original publication information is usually given at the bottom of the first page of the excerpted material.

2. In the preceding entry, the square brackets indicate that the title of the reprinted excerpt from a chapter in Male's book was created by Seymour Gross et al. rather than by the author of the material. Gross et al. created their own title for the material they used from Male's book because they only used a small part of Male's chapter. If Gross et al. had reprinted an entire chapter from the book, they would have used Male's chapter title.

CHAPTER 10

Citing Periodicals

What Is a Periodical?

A periodical is a source that is published periodically (at regular intervals). Most scholarly journals are published quarterly (four times per year), although some are published more or less frequently. Popular magazines are usually published every week (weekly), every two weeks (biweekly), every four weeks (monthly), or every two months (bimonthly). Newspapers are usually published every two weeks (biweekly), once a week, twice a week, or daily.

Citing Scholarly Journal Articles

An Article from a Scholarly Journal with Continuous Pagination

Hoffman, Nancy Jo. "Reading Women's Poetry: The Meaning and Our

    Lives." <u>College English</u> 34 (1974): 48-62.

1. In a journal published quarterly, the volume for a particular year will contain four issues. If the first issue of the year ends with page 275 and the next issue begins with page 276, the journal has continuous pagination.

2. Type quotation marks around the title of the article, and underline the title of the journal.

3. Give the volume number in Arabic numerals followed by one space, and type parentheses around the year of publication. Type a colon and one space after the end parenthesis, and give the first page of the article, type a hyphen, and give the last page of the article followed by a period.

4. You may omit the issue number (number 4) and the month (May 1994) or season (Fall 1995) if the journal's pages will be numbered continuously when all the issues are bound together into one volume at the end of the year. However, if you believe this information will be helpful to your reader or if your professor asks you to do so, you may include the issue, month, or season in your entry: 34.1 (Jan. 1974): 48–62. MLA allows you to give additional information beyond what is required if you believe it will be useful to your readers.

5. If no volume is given, use the issue number in place of the volume number.

6. Omit articles such as *The* at the beginning of a journal title, but retain *The* at the beginning of the title of the journal article.

7. If a title or quotation that should be placed in quotation marks appears within the title of the article you are citing, use single quotation marks around the title of the short story, poem, essay, or quotation, and use double quotation marks around the title of the journal article.

```
"Naturalism in Crane's 'The Open Boat.'"
```

8. Underline the title of a novel or play or the name of a work of art that appears in the title of a journal article.

```
Rose, Jacqueline. "Hamlet--the Mona Lisa of Literature." Criti-

     cal Quarterly 28 (1986): 35-49.
```

An Article from a Scholarly Journal without Continuous Pagination

```
Beckman, Joshua. "My Primary Concern with Time." American Po-

     etry Review 27.2 (1998): 11-14.
```

1. If the journal begins each issue published during the year with page 1, give the issue number as well as the volume number.

2. Use double quotation marks around the title of the article, and underline the title of the journal.

3. After the title, type the volume number, a period and no space, the issue number, one space, the year of publication in parentheses followed by a colon and one space, and the inclusive page numbers of the article.

IF YOU ARE USING A BOUND JOURNAL, YOU MUST BE SURE YOU HAVE FOUND THE CORRECT VOLUME AND ISSUE NUMBER FOR THE ARTICLE YOU ARE CITING. THE TABLE OF CONTENTS FOR EACH ISSUE OF THE JOURNAL WILL GIVE THE TITLE OF THE JOURNAL, THE VOLUME NUMBER, THE ISSUE NUMBER, THE DATE OF PUBLICATION, AND A LIST OF ALL THE ARTICLES CONTAINED IN THAT PARTICULAR ISSUE. MAKE SURE THE ARTICLE YOU ARE CITING IS LISTED IN THE TABLE OF CONTENTS FOR THE VOLUME AND ISSUE YOU ARE CITING.

An Article from a Journal Published in More Than One Series

Ghosh, Amitav. "The March of the Novel through History: The

   Testimony of My Grandfather's Bookcase." <u>Kenyon Review</u> ns

   10 (1998): 13-24.

If a journal has been published in more than one series, give the series designation—*2nd ser., 3rd ser., 4th ser., os* ("old" or "original series"), or *ns* ("new series")—after the title of the journal.

Citing Popular Magazines

An Article from a Popular Monthly or Bimonthly Magazine

Michaud, Ellen. "It's the Little Things That Drive You Crazy."

   <u>Prevention</u> July 1998: 112-19.

1. Give the name(s) of the author(s) followed by a period. For the first author listed, give the last name first.
2. Give the title of the article in double quotation marks followed by a period typed inside the final quotation marks.
3. Give the title of the magazine underlined (**not** followed by a period).
4. Give the month and year of publication followed by a colon and one space.
5. Abbreviate the names of all months except May, June, and July. (MLA recommended abbreviations for months are listed in chapter 22.)
6. Give the first page of the article, a hyphen, and the last page of the article followed by a period.

An Article from a Popular Weekly or Biweekly Magazine

Tresniowski, Alex, et al. "Beneath the Surface." <u>People</u> 15 June

   1998: 56-62.

1. Give the name(s) of the author(s) followed by a period. For the first author listed, give the last name first.
2. Give the title of the article in double quotation marks with a period typed inside the final quotation marks.
3. Give the title of the magazine underlined (**not** followed by a period).

4. Give the day, month, and year followed by a colon and one space.
5. Give the first page of the article, a hyphen, and the last page of the article followed by a period.

Citing Newspaper Articles

A Newspaper Article with an Author Given and Numbered Sections

James, Robert F. "New Trends in Health." <u>New York Times</u> 22 July

1997, late ed., sec. 2: 3+.

Citing the Sections of a Newspaper

Newspapers utilize varying methods of identifying the sections, which complicates the matter of citing newspaper sections correctly.

- **Section Letter and Page Number Given on Each Page: natl. ed.: C10.**
  If each page of the newspaper gives a section letter followed by a page number, give the edition (if there is one) followed by a colon and one space. Then give the section letter and page number followed by a period.

- **Page Number and Section Letter Given on Each Page: city ed.: 10C.**
  If each page of the newspaper gives a page number followed by a section letter, give the edition (if there is one) followed by a colon and one space. Then give the page number and section letter exactly as they appear on the page of the newspaper.

- **Numbered Sections: late ed., sec. 5: 7.**
  If the sections of the newspaper are numbered, give the edition (if there is one) followed by a comma and one space. Then type the abbreviation *sec.*, one space, and the section number followed by a colon and one space. Lastly, give the page number followed by a period.

- **Lettered Sections Not Given on Pages: western ed., sec. C: 7+.**
  If the sections of the newspaper are lettered, but only the page numbers are given on the pages of the newspaper, give the edition (if there is one) followed by a comma and one space. Then type the abbreviation *sec.*, one space, and the section letter followed by a colon and one space. Lastly, give the page number followed by a period. Remember to type a plus sign after the page number if the article skips to another page.

---

1. Omit articles such as *The* when they begin the title of a newspaper.
2. If several editions of a newspaper are printed each day, you must give the edition you are using (*natl. ed.*; *city ed.*; *late ed.*) because different editions contain different articles and the same article might be on a different page in a different edition of the paper. You will find the edition on the front page beside the title of the newspaper.
3. If the article begins on one page and skips to another page (for example, it begins on page 3 and continues on page 12), give the first page number followed by a plus sign and a period: 3+.
4. If the city is not named in the title of the newspaper, give it in square brackets after the title along with the MLA recommended abbreviation for the state, province in Canada, or country if the city is not well known or could be confused with another city. (See chapter 22 for MLA recommended abbreviations for states, Canadian provinces, and countries.) You need not specify the city of publication for well-known, nationally published newspapers such as USA Today or the Wall Street Journal, however.

A Newspaper Article with an Author Given and Lettered Sections

Morgan, Mike. "Top Scholars to Discuss Film Industry." Sun News

    [Myrtle Beach, SC] 16 Feb. 2000: C1+.

1. Give the name of the author of the article, inverted for alphabetizing and followed by a period.
2. Give the title of the article in double quotation marks followed by a period typed inside the final quotation marks.
3. Give the title of the newspaper (underlined) followed by the city of publication in square brackets if that information is not given in the title of the paper. Give the MLA-recommended abbreviation for the state, province in Canada, or country if the city could be confused with another city. (See chapter 22 for a list of abbreviations.)
4. Give the day, month, and year followed by a colon and one space.
5. Give the section letter and page number followed by a plus sign if the article skips to a second page (C1+).

A Newspaper Article with No Author Given and Lettered Sections

"Mario Gets Another Chance at Lemans." Morning Call [Allentown,

    PA] 3 Feb. 2000: C1+.

1. If the writer of the article is not given, begin the entry with the title and alphabetize the article under the first significant word of the title excluding *A, An,* and *The.*
2. The parenthetical citation for this entry would be ("Mario" C1).
3. In this entry, *C* refers to the section, *1* refers to the page number, and the plus sign means that the article begins on page 1 of the section and skips to another page.
4. If the city is not named in the title of the newspaper, give it in square brackets after the title along with the MLA recommended abbreviation for the state, province in Canada, or country if the city is not well known or could be confused with another city. (See chapter 22 for a list of abbreviations.) You need not specify the city of publication for well-known, nationally published newspapers such as the <u>Wall Street Journal</u> or the <u>Chronicle of Higher Education.</u>
5. Use MLA recommended abbreviations for all months except May, June, and July. (See chapter 22 for a list of MLA-recommended abbreviations for months.)

A Daily <u>New York Times</u> Article (Lettered Sections)

Paulson, Sam. "What's Happening in Washington?" <u>New York Times</u>

    4 May 1999, late ed.: C5.

On Monday through Saturday, the <u>New York Times</u> is usually divided into lettered sections, each paginated separately. The section letter and the page number are given together on each page (A3; C6; D9). After the edition, give the section letter and page number together just as found on the pages of the newspaper.

A Saturday <u>New York Times</u> Article (No Sections)

Read, Sally R. "Finding Good Medical Care." <u>New York Times</u> 22

    Aug. 1998, late ed.: 12.

Sometimes the Saturday edition of the <u>New York Times</u> is paginated continuously from the first page to the last. If there are no section numbers, just give the page number(s) after the edition.

A Sunday <u>New York Times</u> Article (Numbered Sections)

Meadows, Michael. "Congress and the Waiting Game." <u>New York</u>

    <u>Times</u> 11 July 1999, late ed., sec. 4: 3+.

The Sunday <u>New York Times</u> contains several numbered sections, each paginated separately. After the date, give the edition, the appropriate section number followed by a colon, one space, and the page number(s). Type a plus sign (+) after the page number if the article skips to another page in the paper.

A Signed Editorial

Goodson, Ralph T. "Voters Must Not Be Ignored." Editorial.

    <u>Washington Post</u> 14 Nov. 1999: A8.

An Unsigned Editorial

"City Officials Must Take a Stand." Editorial. <u>Post and Courier</u>

    [Charleston, SC] 23 June 1998: 10A.

A Letter to the Editor

Stein, Brenda K. Letter. <u>New York Times</u> 24 Feb. 1999, natl.

    ed., sec. 5: 7.

Citing Reviews from Journals, Magazines, and Newspapers

A Review of a Book Taken from a Newspaper

Duncan, Roger P. Rev. of <u>The Fragile Thread: The Meaning of</u>

    <u>Form in Faulkner's Novels</u>, by Donald M. Kartiganer. <u>New</u>

    <u>York Times Book Review</u> 15 Jan. 1981: 12-13.

A Review of a Book Taken from a Scholarly Journal

Martin, Jay. Rev. of <u>Home as Found: Authority and Genealogy in</u>

    <u>Nineteenth-Century American Literature</u>, by Eric J.

    Sundquist. <u>American Literature</u> 52 (1981): 654-55.

A Review of a Television Movie Taken from a Biweekly Popular Magazine

Sheffield, Rob. Rev. of <u>The David Cassidy Story</u>. <u>Rolling Stone</u>

    20 Jan. 2000: 61.

A Review of a Play Taken from a Newspaper

Becker, Harold D., Jr. "New Production Opens to Enthusiastic

    Audience." Rev. of <u>The Glass Menagerie</u>, by Tennessee

    Williams. Morosco Theater, New York. <u>New York Times</u>

    17 July 1994, late ed., sec. 3: 7+.

CHAPTER 11

Citing Miscellaneous Other Sources

A Pamphlet

Smith, Bert Kruger. <u>Women Drinkers</u>. Austin: U of Texas, 1976.

A Government Publication

Thomson, Michael, comp., and John Y. Cole, ed. Library of Congress. <u>Books Change Lives: 1993-1994 Reading Promotion
Campaign</u>. Washington: GPO, 1995.

United States. Subcommittee on Government Information and Regulation of the Committee on Governmental Affairs. <u>A Lesson
of the Gulf War: National Security Requires Computer Secu-
rity</u>. 102nd Cong. 1st sess. Senate Hearing 575. Washington: GPO, 1992.

United States. United States Department of Health and Human
Services. National Institute on Aging. <u>Grow into Growing
Older: Don't Take It Easy--Exercise!</u> Washington: GPO,
1992.

1. Give the author, or editor (*ed.*), or compiler (*comp.*) if these names are available.
2. If no author is listed, give the name of the federal (United States), state (Georgia), city (Boston), or local government responsible for the publication.
3. Next give the name of the agency (or agencies) that published the material. If several government agencies are listed on the publication, give the largest agency first, then the smaller agency.
4. Give the title of the document (underlined).
5. Give the city, publisher, and year of publication (if known). Use the abbreviation *GPO* if the Government Printing Office is the publisher.

An Unpublished Dissertation

```
Franson, Robert T. "Women in Shakespeare's History Plays."

    Diss. U of Southern California, 1988.
```

1. Give the author's name inverted for alphabetizing.
2. Place the title of an unpublished dissertation in double quotation marks.
3. Type the abbreviation *Diss.*, and then give the name of the university where the dissertation was done followed by a comma and one space. Then give the year of completion followed by a period.

A Published Dissertation

```
Gradius, Caroline P. Biblical Imagery in the Novels of Herman

    Melville. Diss. Wake Forest U, 1995. New York: UMI, 1996.

    7865349.
```

1. Give the author's name inverted for alphabetizing.
2. Underline the title of a published dissertation.
3. Type the abbreviation *Diss.*, and then give the name of the university where the dissertation was done followed by a comma and one space. Then give the year of completion followed by a period.
4. Give the city, publisher, and year of publication.
5. If University Microfilms International is the publisher, use the abbreviation UMI.
6. Give the UMI order number if you think it would be helpful to your readers.

An Abstract from Dissertation Abstracts International

```
Graham, Stephen A. "Mirror Imagery in the Poetry of Sylvia

    Plath." Diss. Duke U, 1993. DAI 54 (1993): 1269A.
```

Currently in Dissertation Abstracts International, an *A* after the page number indicates that the dissertation was done in the humanities or social sciences, a *B* indicates that the dissertation was done in engineering or the sciences, and a *C* indicates that the dissertation was done in a university located outside the United States.

An Article from the <u>CQ Researcher</u> (Congressional Quarterly)

Roberts, Jerry S. "The Medicare Issue." <u>CQ Researcher</u> 22 Dec.

1995: 865-87.

An Article from <u>Facts on File</u>

"Conservation Issues Discussed in Washington." <u>Facts on File</u>

<u>World News Digest</u> 24 June 1995: 274-75.

A Film

<u>Gone with the Wind</u>. Dir. Victor Fleming. Prod. David O. Selz-

nick. Screenplay by Sidney Howard. Perf. Vivien Leigh and

Clark Gable. MGM, 1939.

1. Give the title of the film (underlined).
2. Give the director (*Dir.*), the distributor (MGM, Paramount, etc.), and the year the film was released.
3. Give any other information that might be useful to your reader, such as producer (*Prod.*) and performers (*Perf.*), before the distributor. (See the list of MLA-recommended abbreviations in chapter 22.)

A Videocassette or Digital Videodisc (DVD)

<u>Titanic</u>. Perf. Kate Winslet and Leonardo DiCaprio. Dir. James

Cameron. 1997. Videocassette. Paramount, 1998.

<u>Runaway Bride</u>. Perf. Julia Roberts and Richard Gere. Dir. Garry

Marshall. 1999. DVD. Paramount/Touchstone, 1999.

1. Give the title of the videocassette or DVD (underlined).
2. Give the performers, director, and any other information that might be useful to your reader.
3. Give the date the film was originally released to theaters, if known.
4. Type the word *Videocassette* or *DVD* (not in quotation marks and not underlined), followed by a period.

5. Give the distributor, a comma, and the year the videocassette or DVD was released.

A Television Program

```
Burns, Ken, dir. "Gettysburg." The Civil War. PBS. WHMC, Con-

      way, SC. 22 May 1999.

Madame Bovary. By Gustave Flaubert. Perf. Frances O'Connor and

      Greg Wise. 2 episodes. Masterpiece Theatre. PBS. WHMC,

      Conway, SC. 8 Feb.-13 Feb. 2000.

"The Soul Hunter." Babylon 5. TNT. 15 June 1998.
```

1. Give the title of the individual episode (if available) in double quotation marks (e.g., "The Soul Hunter.").
2. Give the title of the program underlined (e.g., Madame Bovary).
3. You may include any other information that might be useful to your reader—author of work being dramatized (By William Faulkner); director (*dir.*); directed by (*Dir.*); narrated by (*Narr.*); performer (*perf.*); performed by (*Perf.*); script written by (*Writ.*); adapted for television by (*Adapt.*); conductor (*cond.*); conducted by (*Cond.*).
4. If the abbreviation comes after the name, as it will when you begin the entry with a person's name, use the abbreviation beginning with the lowercase letter (e.g., Burns, Ken, dir.). If the abbreviation precedes the name, as it will when the person's name is placed after the title of the program, use the abbreviation beginning with the capital letter (e.g., Dir. Ken Burns.).
5. Give the number of episodes in the program if relevant (e.g., 6 episodes).
6. If the program is part of a series such as Masterpiece Theatre, give the title of the series (not in quotation marks and not underlined).
7. Give the network that broadcast the program followed by a period (e.g., ABC, CBS, NBC, PBS, TNT, Arts and Entertainment Network, History Channel, Learning Channel).
8. Give the call letters followed by a comma and one space. Then give the city of the local station (e.g., WHMC, Conway, SC).
9. Give the postal abbreviation for the state if the city is not well known or could be confused with another city.
10. Give the day, month, and year the program was broadcast.
11. If you are citing the transcript of a television program, type *Transcript* at the end of the entry (not in quotation marks and not underlined).

A Television Interview

```
Clinton, Hillary Rodham. Interview with Ted Koppel. Nightline.

     ABC. WCIV, Charleston, SC. 5 Jan. 2000.

Updike, John. Interview. Charlie Rose. PBS. WHMC, Conway, SC.

     12 Feb. 1996.
```

1. Give the name of the person being interviewed, inverted for alphabetizing.
2. Give the title of the interview (if there is one) in double quotation marks with the period inside the final quotation marks.
3. If the interview has no title, type the word *Interview* (not underlined and not in quotation marks) after the name of the person interviewed. Type *with* and give the name of the interviewer (if known).
4. Give the title of the television show (underlined).
5. Give the network.
6. Give the call letters and city of the local station (separated by a comma and one space).
7. Give the date the interview aired on the show.

A Radio Program

```
Brinker, Bob. Moneytalk. WRNN, Myrtle Beach, SC. 14 June 1998.
```

1. Give the name of the host of the show (if there is one), with the name inverted for alphabetizing. (In the citation above, Bob Brinker is the host of a call-in radio show dealing with investment strategies.)
2. Give the title of the individual episode or segment (if there is one) in double quotation marks.
3. Give the name of the narrator (if there is one) preceded by the abbreviation *Narr.* (e.g., Narr. James Earl Jones.) after the title of the episode. (Note: A host is the major focus of the show and would be speaking throughout the show, whereas a narrator might introduce the show, make some explanatory remarks during the show, and make concluding remarks at the end of the show. In other words a host is more central to the show than a narrator would be.)
4. Give the title of the program (underlined).
5. Give the network (if known) (e.g., National Public Radio or NPR).
6. Give the call letters and city of the local station (separated by a comma and one space).

7. Give the postal abbreviation for the state if the city is not well known or could be confused with another city.

8. Give the day, month, and year the program was broadcast.

A Song

Springfield, Rick, comp. and perf. "Jessie's Girl." <u>Working</u>

   <u>Class Dog</u>. LP. RCA, 1981.

1. Give the composer (*comp.*), performer (*perf.*), or conductor (*cond.*), whichever is most important.

2. Place the title of the song in double quotation marks.

3. Underline the title of the compact disc, record, audiocassette, or audiotape.

4. If you do not specify otherwise, the song is assumed to have been recorded on a compact disc. If the song was not recorded on a compact disc, identify the medium as an *LP* (long-playing record), *Audiotape* (reel-to-reel tape), or *Audiocassette* (not underlined and not in quotation marks).

5. Give the manufacturer (e.g., RCA, Capitol, Deutsche Grammophon).

6. Give the year of issue, or type *n.d.* if the date is unavailable.

Song Lyrics from an LP Liner or Compact Disc Booklet

Knopfler, Mark. "Sultans of Swing." Liner. <u>Dire Straits</u>. LP.

   Warner, 1978.

Liner Notes or Booklet Essay from a Record or Compact Disc

DeCurtis, Anthony. "Eric Clapton: A Life at the Crossroads."

   Booklet essay. <u>Crossroads</u>. By Eric Clapton. 4 Compact Disc

   Edition. Polydor, 1988.

1. Give the author of the liner notes or booklet (if available).

2. Give the title of the booklet, booklet essay, or liner notes, in double quotation marks.

3. Give a description of the material—*Booklet, Booklet essay, Liner notes, Libretto*—capitalized (first word only), not underlined and not in quotation marks, followed by a period.

4. Underline the title of the compact disc, record, audiocassette, or audiotape.

5. Type *By* and give the name of the performer or musical group.

6. Unless the work is a compact disc, identify it as an *LP* (long-playing record), *Audiotape* (reel to reel tape), or *Audiocassette* (not underlined and not in quotation marks).

7. Give the number of discs in a multiple disc collection.

8. Give the manufacturer (e.g., RCA, Capitol, Deutsche Grammophon).

9. Give the year of issue, or type *n.d.* if the date is unavailable.

A Music Video

```
Henley, Don. "Taking You Home." Inside Job. Warner Bros., 2000.

      Music video. Dir. Tom Krueger and Mary K. Place. VH1. 23

      Apr. 2000.
```

1. Give the name(s) of the performer(s) of the song.

2. Give the title of the song in double quotation marks.

3. Give the title of the CD, LP, or other medium (underlined).

4. Give the manufacturer (record company), type a comma and one space, and give the date the CD, LP, or other medium was released.

5. Type the words *Music video* (not in quotation marks or underlined and followed by a period).

6. Type the abbreviation *Dir.* and give the name(s) of the person(s) who directed the video. (The director's name and much of the other information you need for your citation will be given at the beginning and again at the end of the video.)

7. Give the channel on which you watched the video.

8. Give the day, month, and year you watched the video.

A Map

```
Alabama and Georgia. Map. Heathrow, FL: American Automobile As-

      sociation, 1995.
```

1. Give the title of the map underlined and followed by a period.

2. Type the word *Map* (not in quotation marks and not underlined) followed by a period.

3. Give the city, publisher, and date of publication.

An Advertisement

```
Marlboro. Philip Morris, Inc. Advertisement. Rolling Stone

    28 May 1999: 104-5.

Woman's Vintage Jean Jacket. GAP Jeans. Advertisement. Rolling

    Stone 2 Mar. 2000: 3-4.
```

1. Give the name of the product (if there is one).
2. Give the name of the company (if available).
3. Type the word *Advertisement* (not underlined and not in quotation marks) followed by a period.
4. Give the publication information. (Rolling Stone in the preceding entry is a popular biweekly magazine.)

A Cartoon

```
Marlette, Doug. "Kudzu." Cartoon. Sun News [Myrtle Beach, SC]

    4 July 1998: C10.
```

1. Give the name of the cartoonist (if available).
2. Give the title of the cartoon (if available) in double quotation marks.
3. Type the word *Cartoon* (not in quotation marks and not underlined) followed by a period.
4. Give the publication information for the newspaper or magazine.

A Poster

```
The Harmful Effects of Steroids. Poster. Bruce Algra's Health

    and Drug Education Series. Bakersfield, CA: Algra, 1992.

Poisonous Snakes of South Carolina. Poster. Cooperative Publi-

    cation of the Greenville Zoo, BiLo, the Endangered

    Wildlife Fund, and the South Carolina Department of Nat-

    ural Resources. N.p.: n.p., n.d.
```

A Poster Published in a Magazine

```
Whales of the World. Poster. National Geographic Dec.

    1976: 722A.
```

1. Give the title of the poster (underlined and followed by a period).
2. Type the word *Poster* (not in quotation marks and not underlined).
3. Give the publication information for the magazine (title, date, page).

A Speech, Lecture, or Presentation

Beard, John. "Metanarratives Be Damned: Teaching the Postmodern

    Student." Back to the Future. College English Association

    Conference. Charleston, SC. 7 Apr. 2000.

Smith, Rachel T. "Using Assessment Strategies in the ESL Class-

    room." South Atlantic Modern Language Association Confer-

    ence. Atlanta, GA. 16 Nov. 1997.

1. Give the speaker's name.
2. Give the title of the presentation in quotation marks.
3. If no title is known, type the appropriate description—*Speech, Keynote address, Lecture, Address, Reading, Presentation* (not underlined and not in quotation marks) followed by a period.
4. Give the name of the meeting for that particular year (if known). (Each year's conference typically has a title.)
5. Give the name of the organization that sponsored the meeting.
6. Give the city in which the conference was held. Give the postal abbreviation for the state if the city is unfamiliar or could be confused with another city (e.g., Charleston, SC; Charleston, WV).
7. Give the day, month, and year the presentation was delivered.

A Published Interview

Rodden, John. "A Harsh Day's Light: An Interview with Marge

    Piercy." <u>Kenyon Review</u> ns 10 (1998): 132-43.

Note that *ns* means *new series*.

A Personal or Telephone Interview

Angelou, Maya. Personal interview. 15 Aug. 1999.

Morrison, Toni. Telephone interview. 18 Aug. 1998.

A Published Letter

Dickinson, Emily. "To Thomas Wentworth Higginson." 15 April

    1862. <u>Selected Poems and Letters of Emily Dickinson</u>. Ed.

    Robert N. Linscott. Garden City, NY: Anchor-Doubleday,

    1959. 291-92.

An Unpublished Letter

Walker, Alice. Letter to the author. 26 Apr. 1999.

CHAPTER 12

Citing Internet Sources

The method of citing electronic sources is constantly changing as the materials available on the Internet change. The Modern Language Association regularly updates citation requirements, so you should be aware that citations you might see in your sources done even a year or two ago may be out of date by now. The guidelines in this text are based on MLA guidelines published in 1999.

Sometimes the Web page you are looking at will not have all the information you need to create your citation. You may have to go to the Web site's home page (the title page or first page of the site) to get some of the information you need, such as the name of the organization sponsoring the site. If you think you might use information from a Web site, make sure you have all the information needed for your works-cited page recorded in your working bibliography before you move on to another site, otherwise you may have to spend time relocating the site later to get what you need.

Because the material on Web sites is constantly being updated, always print out or download any material you think you might need to include in your works-cited list. The information may not be available the next time you visit the site.

General Guidelines for Citing Internet Sources

Include as much of the information listed here as you can find, but realize that you may not find everything for every electronic source. Give your reader enough information to be able to locate the information on the Internet.

1. Give the name of the author, editor (*ed.*), compiler (*comp.*), translator (*trans.*), or person responsible for maintaining the Web site. The name(s) you need will be usually be given on the home page, which is the title page or first page of a Web site from which you access (through hypertext links) the other pages on the site. Invert the name of the first person listed for alphabetizing. Use the appropriate abbreviation after the name if the person was not an author (e.g., Smith, David T., ed.).

2. Give the title in double quotation marks if it is an article from a journal, magazine, or newspaper, or a short story, short poem, essay, book chapter, or other type of work usually identified by double quotation marks.

3. Underline the title of an online book, journal, magazine, or newspaper.

4. If a book has both an author and an editor (*Ed.*), compiler (*Comp.*), or translator (*Trans.*), give the author first, then the title, then the editor, compiler, or translator preceded by the appropriate abbreviation (Jamison, Jerome R. <u>Complete Stories</u>. Ed. Alison E. Wilmot.).

5. Give the city, publisher, and year of publication of the print version of a work (Boston: Houghton, 1989.).

6. Give the volume, issue, year of publication, and total number of pages or paragraphs (if given) for a journal article (34.6 (1998): 9 pp.). Give specific page numbers if they are available (34.6 (1998): 341–49.).

7. Give the month, year, and total number of pages or paragraphs (if given) for a monthly or bimonthly magazine (Jan. 1999: 3 pars.). Give specific page numbers if they are available (Jan. 1999: 24.).

8. Give the title (underlined) of the database, magazine, scholarly journal, newspaper, scholarly project, professional site, or personal site (if that information is available). If no title for the site is given, use a term such as *Home page* (not in quotation marks and not underlined) to identify the type of site you are referring to.

9. Give the date the material was posted to the site or the date of the most recent updating (if available).

10. Give the name of the organization that sponsors the site (if known).

11. Give the date you accessed the site or downloaded or printed out material from the site.

12. Give the electronic address in angle brackets (< >) followed by a period.

Copying the URL Precisely

Be scrupulously accurate when copying the URL (*uniform resource locator* or electronic address) into your citation. One incorrect space or typo will prevent you or anyone else from relocating the Web site.

Creating Parenthetical Citations for Internet Sources

If a Web site has page numbers or paragraph numbers, use them in your parenthetical citations. Many Web documents, however, are not paginated, nor do they have numbered paragraphs. For those documents, you do not have to give a page or paragraph number in your parenthetical citation; just name the author(s) either in your sentence or in the parenthetical citation at the end of your sentence. You may also use the MLA abbreviation *n. pag.* to assure your reader that no pages were given for you to cite.

Some instructors will ask you to turn in photocopies of all print materials and printouts of Web materials cited in your paper. An instructor who is

---

Breaking a URL

In MLA-style documentation, an electronic address may be broken only by typing **one space after a slash.** Do not use a hyphen or any other method to break a URL.

---

checking your citations for accuracy may need you to identify the pages in the Web site printouts from which you quoted, paraphrased, or summarized information. In this case, follow your instructor's guidelines for giving print-out page numbers in your parenthetical citations. MLA allows you to give additional information beyond the minimum requirements if you think such information will be useful to your reader.

A Web Site

McAllister, Jim. "Nathaniel Hawthorne's Neighborhood." <u>Salem,</u>

 <u>Massachusetts: Salem Tales</u>. Jan. 2000. 11 Feb. 2000

 <http://www.salemweb.com/tales/hawthorne1.htm>.

1. Give the name of the person responsible for the Web site (if available). Sometimes only initials will be given. Check the home page (title page) of the site to see if the full name is given there. If a name cannot be found, begin your citation with the title of the page.
2. Give the name of the individual page in double quotation marks with a period inside the final quotation marks.
3. Give the title of the entire Web site of which this page is a small part (underlined and followed by a period). Check the site's home page for this information.
4. Give the date of posting or the date the page was updated. This information is usually given at the end of the material on the Web page.
5. Give the date you accessed, downloaded, or printed out the material.
6. Give the electronic address in angle brackets followed by a period.

An Online Scholarly Database or Project

<u>Women of the Romantic Period</u>. Ed. Daniel Anderson and Morri

 Safran. 3 Nov. 1996. U Texas at Austin. 21 Feb. 2000

 <http://www.cwrl.utexas.edu/~worp/ack.html>.

1. Give the title of the scholarly database or project (underlined).
2. Type *Ed.* ("Edited by") and give the name(s) of the editor(s) of the site.
3. Give the date the site was updated.
4. Give the name of the organization or university that sponsors the site.
5. Give the date you accessed the information on the site.
6. Give the electronic address in angle brackets followed by a period.

Citing Online Books and Parts of Books

A Book Available in Print and Online

Fielding, Henry. A History of Tom Jones, a Foundling. N.p.,

1749. 25 June 1998 <gopher:vt.edu:10010/02/82/1>.

Sandburg, Carl. Chicago Poems. New York: Holt, 1916. 21 Feb.

2000 <http://www.bartleby.com/165/index.html>.

Whitman, Walt. Leaves of Grass. Ed. David McKay. N.p: n.p.,

1900. 18 May 1998 <http://www.columbia.edu/acis/bartleby/

whitman/whit111.html>.

1. Give the author's name, last name first, followed by a period.
2. Give the title of the work (underlined).
3. Give the editor, translator, or compiler if there is one.
4. Give the original publication data (city: publisher, year.) or use the appropriate abbreviations to indicate that the information was not available. If the publication information is not available on the Web site but can be found elsewhere, provide it in square brackets: [Boston: St. Martin's, 1996.].
5. Give the date you accessed the material.
6. Give the electronic address in angle brackets (< >) followed by a period.

An Introduction, Preface, Foreword, or Afterword from an Online Book

McKay, David. Preface. Leaves of Grass. By Walt Whitman. Ed.

McKay. N.p.: n.p., 1900. 25 June 1998 <http://

www.columbia.edu/acis/bartleby/whitman/whit111.html>.

Citing Plays Available in Print and Online

```
O'Neill, Eugene. Beyond the Horizon: A Play in Three Acts. New
    York: Boni, 1920. 21 Feb. 2000 <http://www.bartleby.com/
    br/132.html>.
Sophocles. Oedipus the King. Trans. Francis Storr. Ed. T. E.
    Page and W. H. D. Rouse. London: Heinemann, 1912. UM Text
    Initiative. 1993. 25 June 1998 <http://www.hti.umich.edu/
    bin/pd-idx?type=header&idno=SophoOediK>.
```

1. Give the author's name, last name first, followed by a period.
2. Give the title of the play (underlined).
3. Give the editor, translator, or compiler if there is one.
4. Give the publication data for the printed version of the work.
5. Give the name of the organization responsible for publishing the online version of the work.
6. Give the date of electronic publication.
7. Give the date you accessed the material.
8. Give the electronic address in angle brackets followed by a period.

Citing Online Scholarly Journals

An Article from an Online Scholarly Journal (E-Journal)

```
DeShong, Scott. "Sylvia Plath, Emmanuel Levinas, and the Aes-
    thetics of Pathos." Postmodern Culture 8.3 (1998): 23
    pars. 25 June 1998 <http://www.iath.virginia.edu/pmc/
    current.issue/8.3deshong.html>.
```

1. Give the author's name, inverted for alphabetizing.
2. Give the title of the article in double quotation marks.
3. Give the title of the scholarly journal (underlined).
4. Give the volume number, a period, and the issue number (if given) followed by the year of publication in parentheses, and a colon.
5. Give the total number of pages, paragraphs, or sections (if available).

6. Give the date you accessed the article.

7. Give the electronic address in angle brackets followed by a period.

A Book Review from an Online Scholarly Journal

Plotnitsky, Arkady. "The Cosmic Internet." Rev. of <u>The Life of</u>

   <u>the Cosmos</u>, by Lee Smolin. <u>Postmodern Culture</u> 8.3 (1998):

   34 pars. 25 June 1998 <http://www.iath.virginia.edu./pmc/

   current.issue/8.3.r-plotnitsky.html>.

A Journal Article Reprinted on a Professor's University Home Page

Ewert, Jeanne. "Deep and Dark Waters: Raymond Chandler Revisits

   the Fin-de-Siècle." <u>Genre</u> 27.3 (1994): 255-74. Jeanne

   Ewert's Home Page. School of Literature, Communication,

   and Culture. Georgia Institute of Technology. 2 Sept. 1999

   <http://www.lcc.gatech.edu/~ewert/papers/darkwaters/

   index.html>.

Citing Online Popular Magazines

An Online Monthly or Bimonthly Magazine Article

Kurzweil, Raymond. "Live Forever: Uploading the Human Brain."

   <u>Psychology Today Online</u> Jan. 2000: n. pag. 30 Jan. 2000

   <http://www.psychologytoday.com/features3.html>.

Stark, Steven. "The First Postmodern Presidency." <u>Atlantic</u>

   <u>Monthly</u> April 1993: n. pag. 30 Jan. 2000 <http://

   www.theatlantic.com/politics/polibig/postmod.htm>.

1. Give the author's name (if known).

2. Give the title of the article in double quotation marks followed by a period inside the final quotation marks.

3. Give the title of the magazine (underlined and not followed by a period).
4. Give the month and year the article was published, type a colon and give the total number of pages or paragraphs (if known) (6 pp.; 23 pars.). If the article has no page numbers or numbered paragraphs, use *n. pag.* to indicate that the article had no pagination.
5. For a bimonthly magazine, give both months (Jan.-Feb. 2000).
6. Do not give the volume and issue numbers even if that information is available.
7. Give the date you accessed, downloaded, or printed out the article.
8. Give the electronic address in angle brackets followed by a period.

An Online Weekly or Biweekly Magazine Article

```
Thompson, Dick. "The Gene Machine." Time 24 Jan. 2000: n. pag.

    30 Jan. 2000 <http://pathfinder.com/time/magazine/

    articles/0,3266,37624,00.html>.
```

1. Give the author's name (if known).
2. Give the title of the article in double quotation marks followed by a period inside the final quotation marks.
3. Give the title of the magazine (underlined and not followed by a period).
4. Give the day, month, and year the article was published, type a colon and give the specific page numbers (if known) or the total number of pages or paragraphs (if known) (6 pp.; 23 pars.). Type *n. pag.* if the article has no pagination.
5. Do not give the volume and issue numbers for a weekly or biweekly magazine.
6. Give the date you accessed the article, downloaded, or printed out the article.
7. Give the electronic address in angle brackets followed by a period.

Citing Online Newspaper Articles

A Newspaper Article Available Online

```
Greenhouse, Steven. "Companies React Quickly to Court's Sexual

    Harassment Rulings." New York Times on the Web 28 June

    1998. 28 June 1998 <http://www.nytimes.com/yr/mo/day/news/

    washpol/scotus-harass.html>.
```

1. Give the author's name (inverted) if available.
2. If no author is given, begin the entry with the title of the article and alphabetize the entry by the first significant word of the title excluding *A*, *And*, and *The*.
3. Give the title of the article in double quotation marks.
4. Give the title of the online newspaper (underlined).
5. Give the date of electronic publication.
6. Give the date you accessed the article, downloaded, or printed out the article.
7. Give the electronic address in angle brackets followed by a period.

A Book Review Taken from an Online Newspaper

Berne, Suzanne. "The Trillin Bunch." Rev. of <u>Family Man</u>, by

Calvin Trillin. <u>New York Times on the Web</u> 21 June 1998.

25 June 1998 <http://www.nytimes.com/books/98/06/21/

reviews/980621.21berne.html>.

A Movie Review Taken from an Online Newspaper

Weintraub, Bernard. "Restoring a Classic: Scarlett, Rhett and

the Old South at Their Most Colorful." Rev. of <u>Gone with</u>

<u>the Wind</u>, dir. Victor Fleming. <u>New York Times on the Web</u>

25 June 1998. 25 June 1998 <http://www.nytimes.com/yr/mo/

day/news/arts/film-gone-wind-restore.html>.

A Review of a Ballet, Opera, Concert, or Play Taken from an Online Newspaper

"Like Shakespeare with Wings, an Airy <u>Midsummer Night's Dream</u>."

Rev. of <u>A Midsummer Night's Dream</u>, by William Shakespeare.

Chor. George Balanchine. New York City Ballet. New York

State Theater, New York. <u>New York Times on the Web</u> 25 June

1998. 25 June 1998 <http://www.nytimes.com/yr/mo/day/

news/arts/dream-ballet-review.html>.

Citing Other Miscellaneous Internet Sources

An E-Mail Message

Smith, Daniel K. "Re: Class Reunion." E-mail to Sandra P.

    Schneider. 28 Feb. 1998.

1. Give the name of the writer of the electronic mail, inverted.
2. Give the title of the message (taken from the subject line) in double quotation marks.
3. Type *E-mail to the author.* or *E-mail to* (name of recipient).
4. Give the day, month, and year of the message.

An Online Posting to an E-Mail Discussion Group, Listserv, or Newsgroup

Fain, Margaret. "New MLA Citation Style for Subscription Data-

    bases." Online posting. 2 Mar. 2000. LIBREF-T. 26 Apr.

    2000 <http://listserv.kent.edu/scripts/

    wa.exe?A2=ind0003A&L=libref-l&P=R1122>.

McCarty, Willard. "One More Than Ten." Online posting. 7 May

    1998. Humanist Discussion Group. 2 July 1998 <http://

    lists.village.virginia.edu/lists_archive/Humanist/v12/

    0001.html>.

1. Give the author's name, inverted for alphabetizing.
2. Give the title of the document (in quotation marks) taken from the subject line of the posting.
3. Identify the material as an *Online posting.*
4. Give the date of posting.
5. Give the name of the online discussion group, Listserv, or newsgroup.
6. Give the date you accessed the material.
7. Give the electronic address in angle brackets (or the e-mail address of the moderator of the discussion group) followed by a period.
8. If possible, cite an archived version of the posting, which will make it easier for your readers to find your source if they should wish to do so.

A Forwarded Online Posting to an E-Mail Discussion Group or Listserv

Reynolds, Catherine. "Concert Schedule Update." 3 Feb. 2000.

Fwd. by Susan Groves. Online posting. 5 Feb. 2000.

Rick Springfield OneList. 7 Feb. 2000 <http://

www.sunshinesmiley.com/rickspringfield/>.

1. Give the name of the author of the original e-mail, inverted.
2. Give the title of the document (in quotation marks) taken from the subject line of the e-mail message.
3. Give the date the original message was posted.
4. Type *Fwd. by* ("forwarded by"), and give the name of the person who forwarded the message.
5. Identify the material as an *Online posting*.
6. Give the date the message was forwarded.
7. Give the name of the online discussion group or Listserv.
8. Give the date you accessed the material.
9. Give the electronic address of the discussion group in angle brackets (or the e-mail address of the moderator of the group) followed by a period.

A Professional Site

Coastal Carolina University Home Page. 15 Dec. 1999. 26 Apr.

2000 <http://www.coastal.edu/>.

Home Page. Office of Elementary and Secondary Education. United

States Dept. of Education. 24 Jan. 2000. 30 Jan. 2000

<http://www.ed.gov/offices/OESE/index.html>.

1. Give the name(s) of the author(s) of the home page if available.
2. Give the name of the site (underlined), or if no site name is available, type *Home page* (not in quotation marks and not underlined). The home page is the title page or first page of a Web site from which you access (through hypertext links) the other pages on the site.
3. Give the name of the organization responsible for the home page (if available), not underlined. You may omit this information if the site name contains the name of the organization sponsoring the site.

4. Give the date material on the page was updated (if available).
5. Give the date you accessed the material.
6. Give the electronic address in angle brackets followed by a period.

A Personal Site

Halfacre, Kandice. <u>Angel Project</u>. 24 Jan. 2000 <http://

    www.geocities.com/TelevisionCity/Taping/1702/

    angelproject.html>.

O'Neal, Kristy, Carrie Ryan, and Michael Duncan. <u>South Carolina

    Hootie Home Page</u>. 15 May 1998 <http://s9000.furman.edu/

    ~oneal/hootie/yahoo.html>.

1. Give the name of the person who created the site, inverted for alphabetizing, and followed by a period.
2. Give the title of the site if there is one, underlined and followed by a period. If the site has no title, type *Home page,* not underlined and not in
   quotation marks, followed by a period.
3. Give the date you accessed the site.
4. Give the electronic address in angle brackets followed by a period.

An Online Government Publication

United States. Dept. of Education. Office of Elementary and

    Secondary Education. <u>Educational Excellence for All Chil-

    dren Act of 1999: Fact Sheet</u>. 25 May 1999. 30 Jan. 2000

    <http://www.ed.gov/offices/OESE.ESEA/factsheet.html>.

1. Give the author, editor (*ed.*), or compiler (*comp.*) if available.
2. If no author is listed, give the name of the federal (United States), state
   (Georgia), city (Charleston, WV), or local government responsible for
   the publication.
3. Next give the name of the agency (or agencies) that published the material. If several government agencies are listed, give the largest agency
   first, then the smaller agency.
4. Give the title of the document (underlined).

5. Give the date the document was updated (usually found at the end of the document).

6. Give the date you accessed the document.

7. Give the electronic address in angle brackets followed by a period.

An Online Cartoon

Stossel, Sage. "Good Grief!" Cartoon. <u>Atlantic Unbound</u> 5 Jan.

    2000. 30 Jan. 2000 <http://www.theatlantic.com/unbound/

    sage/ss2000-01-05.htm>.

1. Give the name of the person who created the cartoon (if known).

2. Give the title of the cartoon (if known) in double quotation marks.

3. Type the word *Cartoon,* neither in quotation marks nor underlined. If no cartoonist or title is known, begin the entry with the word *Cartoon.*

4. Give the title of the online magazine or newspaper (underlined).

5. Give the date the cartoon was published.

6. Give the date you accessed the cartoon on the Internet.

7. Give the electronic address in angle brackets followed by a period.

An Online Illustration

"The June 10, 1692 Hanging of Bridget Bishop." Illustration.

    <u>Images from the Salem Witchcraft Trials</u>. 11 Feb. 2000

    <http://www.law.umkc.edu/faculty/projects/ftrials/salem/

    SAL_IHAN.HTM>.

1. Give the title of the illustration in double quotation marks followed by a period inside the final quotation mark.

2. Type the word *Illustration,* not in quotation marks and not underlined.

3. Give the title of the Web site, underlined and followed by a period.

4. Give the date the Web site was last updated (if known).

5. Give the date you accessed the illustration on the Web site.

6. Give the electronic address in angle brackets followed by a period.

An Online Photograph

McAllister, Jim. "House of the Seven Gables." Photograph.

Salem, Massachusetts: Salem Tales. Jan. 2000. 11 Feb. 2000

<http://www.salemweb.com/tales/hawthorne1.htm>.

1. Give the name of the photographer (if available).
2. Give the title of the photograph in double quotation marks.
3. Type the word *Photograph* (not in quotation marks and not under-lined) followed by a period.
4. Give the name of the Web site underlined and followed by a period.
5. Give the date the site was last updated (if known).
6. Give the date you accessed, downloaded, or printed out the photograph.
7. Give the electronic address in angle brackets followed by a period.

An Online Map

"Salem in 1692: Town and Village." Map. Images from the Salem

Witch Trials. 11 Feb. 2000 <http://www.law.umkc.edu/

faculty/projects/ftrials/salem/SAL_MAP.HTM>.

1. Give the title of the map, in double quotation marks.
2. Type the word *Map,* not in quotation marks and not underlined.
3. Give the title of the Web site, underlined and followed by a period.
4. Give the date the Web site was updated (if available). Note that in the citation above, no date of last updating was given on the Web site. Therefore the date could not be cited in the entry. You are not obligated to give information that is not available to you on the site.
5. Give the date you accessed the map.
6. Give the electronic address in angle brackets followed by a period.

An Online Radio Program

Brinker, Bob. Moneytalk with Bob Brinker. KGO, San Francisco.

19 Feb. 2000. <http://www.bobbrinker.com/webstations.asp>.

1. Give the name of the host of the show. If the show had a narrator (*narr.*) or performer (*perf.*) rather than a host, follow the name with the appropriate abbreviation (e.g., Sutherland, Donald, narr.).
2. Give the title of the individual episode (if there is one) in double quotation marks.
3. Give the title of the program (underlined).
4. Give the call letters and city of the local station.
5. Give the postal abbreviation for the state if the city is not well known or could be confused with another city.
6. Give the day, month, and year the program was broadcast.
7. Give the electronic address of the site from which you accessed the broadcast.

A Radio Program Accessed from an Online Archive

```
Brinker, Bob. Moneytalk with Bob Brinker. 13 Feb. 2000. KXL

     Moneytalk Archive. 18 Feb. 2000 <http://www.broadcast.com/

     radio/archives/KXL/brinker/>.
```

1. Give the name of the host of the show. If the show had a narrator (*narr.*) or performer (*perf.*) rather than a host, follow the name with the appropriate abbreviation (e.g., Rickman, Alan, narr.).
2. Give the title of the individual episode in double quotation marks (if available).
3. Give the title of the program (underlined).
4. Give the day, month, and year the program was originally broadcast.
5. Give the name of the Web site from which the program was accessed (underlined).
6. Give the date you accessed the archived broadcast of the program.
7. Give the electronic address of the site from which you accessed the broadcast.

Downloaded Computer Software

```
Adobe Acrobat. Vers. 3.01. 25 June 1998 <http://cgi1.adobe.com/

     acrobat/download6.cgi>.
```

1. Give the name of the software.
2. Give the version (if available).
3. Give the date you downloaded the software.
4. Give the electronic address in angle brackets followed by a period.

CHAPTER 13

Citing Materials from Reference Databases

Citing Articles from Reference Books

A Signed Article in a Frequently Republished General Encyclopedia or Well-Known Reference Book

Thomas, Jonathan R. "Clemens, Samuel Langhorne." <u>The New Encyclopaedia Britannica: Macropaedia</u>. 15th ed. 1998.

1. Give the author's name, inverted for alphabetizing. Look for the author's name at the end of the article. If the author's initials are given at the end of the article, look for the full name in a list of contributors at the beginning of the reference book.
2. Give the title of the article (in double quotation marks) exactly as it appears in the encyclopedia—names inverted for alphabetizing.
3. Give the title of the encyclopedia or reference book (underlined).
4. For <u>New Encyclopaedia Britannica</u>, type a colon after the title and specify whether your article came from the Micropaedia section, which gives short articles, or the Macropaedia section, which gives longer articles.
5. Give only the edition number and the date of publication for familiar reference books that frequently appear in newly updated editions. Check the copyright page to see whether the work has been frequently republished, or check the edition number. If the work is a fifteenth edition, it has obviously been updated many times.

   If no edition number is given on the title page and only one publication date is given on the copyright page, give full publication information as described in the entries that follow.
6. You may give the year of the edition rather than the edition number and the year (1998 ed.) if the edition number is not specified on the title page.
7. If a frequently republished reference book is organized alphabetically, you may omit the volume and page numbers.

An Unsigned Article in a Frequently Republished General Encyclopedia or Well-Known Reference Book

"Miller, Henry (Valentine)." <u>The New Encyclopaedia Britannica: Micropaedia</u>. 15th ed. 1998.

109

1. If no author is given, begin your entry with the title of the article (in double quotation marks) exactly as it appears in the encyclopedia—names inverted for alphabetizing.

2. Give the title of the encyclopedia or reference book (underlined).

3. For the <u>New Encyclopaedia Britannica</u>, type a colon after the title and specify whether your article came from the Micropaedia section, which gives short articles, or the Macropaedia section, which gives longer articles.

4. Give only the edition number and the date of publication for familiar reference books that frequently appear in newly updated editions. Check the copyright page to see whether the work has been frequently republished, or check the edition number. If the work is a fifteenth edition, it has obviously been updated many times.

   If no edition number is given on the title page and only one publication date is given on the copyright page, give full publication information as described in the entries that follow.

5. You may give the year of the edition rather than the edition number and the year (1998 ed.) if the edition number is not specified on the title page.

6. If the reference book is organized alphabetically, you may omit the volume and page numbers.

A Signed Article in a Subject-Specific Reference Book That Has Appeared in Only One Edition, such as <u>American Writers</u> or <u>British Writers</u>

O'Connor, William Van. "William Faulkner." <u>American Writers: A</u>

    <u>Collection of Literary Biographies</u>. Ed. Leonard Unger.

    Vol. 2. New York: Scribner's, 1974. 54-76.

Sanforth, Henry T. "Ernest Hemingway." <u>American Writers: A Col-</u>

    <u>lection of Literary Biographies</u>. Ed. Leonard Unger. Sup-

    plement 4: Part 1. New York: Scribner's, 1988. 86-98.

Scott-James, R. A., and C. Day Lewis. "Thomas Hardy." <u>British</u>

    <u>Writers</u>. Ed. Ian Scott-Kilvert. Vol. 6. New York: Scrib-

    ner's, 1983. 1-22.

1. Give full publication information for reference books that have appeared in only one edition (no edition number is given on the title page and only one date of publication is given on the copyright page).

2. Give the author(s) name(s) followed by a period. The name of first author listed should be inverted for alphabetizing.

3. Give the title of the article (in double quotation marks) exactly as it appears in the reference book.

4. Give the title of the reference book (underlined).

5. Type the abbreviation *Ed.* ("Edited by") and give the name(s) of the editor(s) with no comma separating the names.

6. Type the abbreviation *Vol.* and give the number of the volume you used.

7. Give the city, publisher, and year of publication.

8. Give the first page of the article, type a hyphen, and give the last page of the article (including the bibliography if there is one).

NOTE THAT IN <u>AMERICAN WRITERS</u>, THE AUTHOR'S NAME IS USUALLY GIVEN AFTER THE BIBLIOGRAPHY ON THE LAST PAGE OF THE ARTICLE.

A Signed Article from <u>Dictionary of Literary Biography</u>

Griffin, Farah Jasmine. "Gwendolyn Brooks." <u>American Poets</u>
<u>Since World War II</u>. Ed. Joseph Conte. Vol. 165 of <u>Dictionary of Literary Biography</u>. Detroit: Bruccoli-Gale, 1996.
81-91.

Harding, Walter. "Henry David Thoreau." <u>The American Renaissance in New England</u>. Ed. Joel Myerson. Vol. 1 of <u>Dictionary of Literary Biography</u>. Detroit: Gale, 1978. 170-82.

1. Each volume of the <u>Dictionary of Literary Biography</u> has a separate title and editor.

2. Give the author of the essay, the title of the essay in double quotation marks, and the title of the volume you are using (underlined) and followed by a period.

3. Type the abbreviation *Ed.* ("Edited by") and give the editor (or editors) of the volume you are using followed by a period.

4. Give the volume and title of the reference series.

5. Give the publication information for the volume you used.

6. Give the first page of the essay, a hyphen, and the last page of the essay (including the bibliography if there is one) followed by a period.

An Excerpt from a Scholarly Journal Article Reprinted in Twentieth-Century Literary Criticism

Heilman, Robert. "The Turn of the Screw as Poem." University of
    Kansas City Review 14.4 (1948): 277-89. Rpt. in Twentieth-
    Century Literary Criticism. Ed. Dennis Poupard. Vol. 24.
    Detroit: Gale, 1987. 336-40.

An Excerpt from an Essay in an Essay Collection Reprinted in Nineteenth-Century Literature Criticism

Loomis, Roger Sherman. "A Defense of Naturalism." Documents of
    Modern Literary Realism. Ed. George J. Becker. Princeton,
    NJ: Princeton UP, 1963. 535-48. Rpt. in Nineteenth-Century
    Literature Criticism. Ed. Joann Cerrito. Vol. 36. Detroit:
    Gale, 1993. 311-16.

An Excerpt from a Scholarly Journal Article Reprinted in Short Story Criticism

Fiedler, Leslie A. "William Faulkner: An American Dickens."
    Commentary 10.4 (1950): 384-87. Short Story Criticism:
    Excerpts from Criticism of the Works of Short Fiction
    Writers. Ed. Laurie Lanzen Harris and Sheila Fitzgerald.
    Vol. 1. Detroit: Gale, 1988. 151.

An Excerpt from an Essay in an Essay Collection Reprinted in Short Story Criticism

West, Ray B., Jr. "Atmosphere and Theme in Faulkner's 'A Rose
    for Emily.'" William Faulkner: Four Decades of Criticism.
    Ed. Linda Welshimer Wagner. [Lansing]: Michigan State UP,
    1973. 192-98. Rpt. in Short Story Criticism: Excerpts
    from Criticism of the Works of Short Fiction Writers.

```
Ed. Laurie Lanzen Harris and Sheila Fitzgerald. Vol. 1.

Detroit: Gale, 1988. 148-51.
```

Citing a Definition from a Dictionary

```
"Lace." Def. 2a. American Heritage Dictionary. 2nd College ed.

    1985.

"Symbolism." New Merriam-Webster Dictionary. 1989 ed.
```

1. Type the word (capitalized and in quotation marks).
2. If the dictionary lists more than one definition and you are referring to only one of those definitions, type the abbreviation *Def.* ("definition"), and give the number and letter (if there is one) of the definition to which you are referring.
3. The parenthetical citation for the first entry would be ("Lace," def. 2a).
4. The parenthetical citation for the second entry would be ("Symbolism").

Citing an Article from SIRS (Social Issues Resources Series) (Print Version)

Social Issues Resources Series (SIRS) is a loose-leaf collection of reprinted magazine and newspaper articles. Each volume of the series presents material related to a single topic of interest to researchers (e.g., The AIDS Crisis, Alcohol, Education, Health, Women, Youth). Check your library's Web site to see if the online version of SIRS is also available.

A Monthly or Bimonthly Magazine Article Reprinted in SIRS

```
Holden, Constance. "Alcoholism and the Medical Cost Crunch."

    Science Mar. 1987: 1132-33. Alcohol. Ed. Eleanor Gold-

    stein. Vol. 2. Boca Raton: SIRS, 1989. Art. 7.
```

1. Give the original publication information for the article. Then give the name of the volume you used in SIRS (underlined), the editor, the volume number, and the publication information on SIRS. Then give the article number using the abbreviation *Art.*
2. Note that an abbreviation that follows a period is always capitalized, whereas abbreviations that do not follow periods begin with lowercase

letters. (See chapter 22 for more information on MLA-recommended abbreviations.).

3. The parenthetical citation for this entry would be (Holden, art. 7).

A Weekly or Biweekly Magazine Article Reprinted in SIRS

Gelman, David, et al. "Treating Teens in Trouble." <u>Newsweek</u> 20

    Jan. 1986: 52+. <u>Youth</u>. Ed. Eleanor Goldstein. Vol. 3. Boca

    Raton: Social Issues Resources Series, 1989. Art. 3.

1. The parenthetical citation for this entry would be (Gelman, art. 3).
2. If you are not certain your reader will recognize a commonly abbreviated publisher's name (*SIRS* for *Social Issues Resources Series, Inc.; MLA* for *Modern Language Association of America; GPO* for *Government Printing Office*), give the publisher's name in full or use a more recognizable abbreviation—*Mod. Lang. Assn.* instead of *MLA,* for example.

A Newspaper Article with an Author Given Reprinted in SIRS

Luber, Kristin. "The Wars between Women." <u>Washington Post</u> 26

    Aug. 1984: C1+. <u>Women</u>. Ed. Eleanor Goldstein. Vol. 6. Boca

    Raton: SIRS, 1989. Art. 13.

The parenthetical citation for this entry would be (Luber, art. 13).

Citing Microform Databases

A Newspaper Article with an Author Given Reprinted in NewsBank (Microform Version)

Bryan, Robert K. "Counseling Children about Aids." <u>San Fran-

    cisco Examiner</u> 22 Jan. 1988: n. pag. <u>NewsBank: Health</u> 11

    (1988): fiche 1, grids B4-7.

1. Give the author(s) of the article, first author's name inverted.
2. Give the title of the article in double quotation marks.
3. Give the title of the newspaper (underlined).

4. If the city of publication is not included in the title of the paper, give it in square brackets after the title. Give the postal abbreviation for the state if the city is not well known or could be confused with another city.

5. Give the day, month, and year of publication followed by a colon and one space and the section and page numbers of the article.

6. If no section and page numbers are given, use the abbreviation *n. pag.*

7. Type <u>NewsBank</u> (underlined), a colon and one space (underlined), and give the title of the section of <u>NewsBank</u> (underlined).

8. Give the volume number. Then give the year in parentheses followed by a colon and one space.

9. Give the fiche number followed by a comma and one space. Then give the grid numbers followed by a period.

10. A parenthetical citation for this entry would be (Bryan, grid B5).

A Newspaper Article with No Author Given Reprinted in <u>NewsBank</u> (Microform Version)

"Problems with Today's Health Care System." <u>Washington Post</u>

    23 June 1991: n. pag. <u>NewsBank: Health</u> 11 (1991): fiche 3,

    grids C6-8.

1. If no author is given, begin your entry with the title of the article in double quotation marks with the period typed inside the final quotation mark.

2. Give the title of the newspaper (underlined).

3. If the city of publication is not included in the title of the paper, give it in square brackets after the title. Give the postal abbreviation for the state if the city is not well known or could be confused with another city.

4. Give the day, month, and year of publication followed by a colon and one space and the section and page numbers of the article.

5. If no section and page numbers are given, use the abbreviation *n. pag.*

6. Type <u>NewsBank</u> (underlined), a colon and one space (underlined), and give the title of the section of <u>NewsBank</u> (underlined).

7. Give the volume number. Then give the year in parentheses followed by a colon and one space.

8. Give the fiche number followed by a comma and one space. Then give the grid numbers.

9. The parenthetical citation for this entry would be ("Problems," grid C7).

Citing CD-ROM Databases

An Entry from an Encyclopedia on CD-ROM

"Frost, Robert Lee." <u>Encarta '95</u>. CD-ROM. Redmond, WA: Mi-
    crosoft, 1995.

A Scholarly Journal Article from <u>ERIC</u> (Educational Resources Information Center) on CD-ROM

Kim, Anna Charr. "How College Faculty Evaluate Second Language
    Writing." <u>Research and Teaching in Developmental Education</u>
    14.1 (1997): 35-48. Abstract. <u>ERIC</u>. CD-ROM. SilverPlatter.
    1992-March 1998. EJ557280.

A Published Dissertation from <u>ERIC</u> on CD-ROM

Unger, Thomas C. <u>Involving ESL Students in American Culture</u>
    <u>through Participation in Private School Activities</u>. Diss.
    Nova Southeastern U, 1997. Abstract. <u>ERIC</u>. CD-ROM. Silver-
    Platter. 1992-March 1998. ED412745.

1. Give the author(s), with the first author's name inverted for alphabetizing.
2. Type double quotation marks around the title of a journal, magazine,
   or newspaper article, or an unpublished dissertation. Underline the
   title of a published dissertation.
3. If the article has been previously published, give the publication
   information.
4. For a dissertation, type the word *Diss.* and give the name of the university where the dissertation was written, followed by a comma, one
   space, and the year of completion.
5. After the original publication information, type either *Full-text* or *Abstract* to let your reader know whether you accessed the entire article
   or dissertation or a brief summary (unless the title of the database indicates that all the materials are abstracts).
6. Give the title of the database (underlined) — <u>ERIC</u>, <u>Dissertation Abstracts Ondisc</u>, <u>New York Times Ondisc</u>, and so on.

7. Identify the medium you used as a CD-ROM (compact disc read-only memory).

8. If you took information from more than one disc of a multiple-disc database, give the total number of discs: CD-ROM. 6 discs.

9. If you took information from only one of several discs, give the number of the disc you used: CD-ROM. Disc 4.

10. Give the name of the vendor or provider (Gale Group, SilverPlatter, UMI-ProQuest, Information Access, Congressional Information Service, Dataware Technologies, etc.). You can usually find the provider's name on the title page of the database. If you have trouble finding this information, ask a librarian to help you.

11. Give the date of electronic publication.

12. Give the item number (if available).

Citing Subscription Online Databases

Your library pays a fee to allow students and faculty access to a number of online databases. Check your library's Web site for access to these databases.

A Scholarly Journal Article from Expanded Academic ASAP

Hall, Christine C., and Matthew J. Crum. "Women and 'Body-

isms' in Television Beer Commercials." Sex Roles: A

Journal of Research 31.5-6 (1994): 329-37. Full-text.

InfoTrac: Expanded Academic ASAP. Online. Gale Group.

Kimbel Library, Conway, SC. 11 Feb. 2000 <http://

web6.infotrac.galegroup.com>.

1. Give the author's full name (inverted for alphabetizing). If there are two or more authors, invert only the name of the first author listed.

2. Give the title of the article in double quotation marks with a period inside the final quotation marks.

3. Give the title of the journal (underlined, not followed by a period).

4. Give the volume number, a period, and the issue number (if given), one space, and the year of publication in parentheses followed by a colon, one space, and the inclusive page numbers of the original publication. (If you are citing a monthly/bimonthly or weekly/biweekly popular magazine rather than a scholarly journal, see the model citations which follow.)

5. After the original publication information, type either *Full-text* or *Abstract* to inform your reader whether you accessed the entire article or just a brief description of the article.

6. Give the name of the database (underlined). If you are using a small database which is a part of a much larger database, give the name of the large database first, type a colon and one space, and give the name of the smaller database: InfoTrac: Expanded Academic ASAP. For example, Expanded Academic ASAP, Health Reference Center, and General BusinessFile are InfoTrac databases offered to libraries for a subscription fee by Gale Group. MasterFILE Premier and Academic Search Elite are two of the EBSCOhost databases offered to libraries for a subscription fee by EBSCOhost Information Services. Look for the name of the larger database on the left side of the home page screen and also in the URL for the database.

7. Give the medium: *Online* (capitalized, but not underlined).

8. Give the name of the provider (the company that makes the database available). For Expanded Academic ASAP, the provider is Gale Group. For EBSCOhost: MasterFile Premier, the provider is EBSCOhost Information Services. Look on the home page of the database and in the URL to find the name of the provider.

9. If you accessed the database through the Web page of a library, give the name of the library followed by a comma and one space. Then give the city in which the library is located followed by a comma, one space, and the postal abbreviation for the state if the city is unfamiliar or could be confused with another city.

10. Give the date you accessed or printed out the material.

11. Give the electronic address of the home or title page of the database in angle brackets followed by a period. (This will be the URL on the page where you began your search by using the database.)

A Monthly Magazine Article from Expanded Academic ASAP

Pleasant, Barbara. "In Celebration of Sweet Potatoes." Organic Gardening Jan. 2000: 32+. Full-text. InfoTrac: Expanded Academic ASAP. Online. Gale Group. Kimbel Library, Conway, SC. 5 May 2000 <http://web5.infotrac.galegroup.com>.

1. If your source is a monthly or bimonthly popular magazine rather than a scholarly journal, do not give the volume and issue numbers even if they are available. Instead, after the title of the magazine (underlined and not followed by a period), give the month (abbreviated except for May, June, and July) and year of publication, type a colon and one space, and give the pages from the beginning to the end of the article. If

only the first page is given for an article that is obviously longer than one page, type a plus sign after the page number. Use the abbreviation *n. pag.* if no page references are given.

2. Then follow the directions given in the preceding entry for citing an online subscription database.

A Weekly Magazine Article from Expanded Academic ASAP

Sancton, Thomas, and Scott Macleod. "The Final Hours: The

Deaths of Princess Diana and Dodi Fayed." Time 16 Feb.

1998: 74-79. Full-text. InfoTrac: Expanded Academic ASAP.

Online. Gale Group. Kimbel Library, Conway, SC. 2 May 2000

<http://web5.infotrac.galegroup.com>.

1. If your source is a weekly or biweekly popular magazine, do not give the volume and issues numbers even if they are available. Instead, after the title of the magazine (underlined and not followed by a period), give the day, month, and year of publication, type a colon and one space, and give the pages from the beginning to the end of the article. If only the first page is given for an article that is obviously longer than one page, type a plus sign after the page number. Use the abbreviation *n. pag.* if no page references are given.

2. Then follow the directions given on pages 117–18 for citing an online subscription database.

A Monthly Magazine Article from Health Reference Center

"Getting the Skinny on TV." Discover Dec. 1999: 34. Full-text.

InfoTrac: Health Reference Center. Online. Gale Group.

Kimbel Library, Conway, SC. 17 Feb. 2000 <http://

web7.infotrac.galegroup.com>.

A Definition from a Dictionary from Health Reference Center

"Body Image." Mosby's Medical, Nursing, and Allied Health Dic-

tionary. 1998 ed. Full-text. InfoTrac: Health Reference

Center. Online. Gale Group. Kimbel Library, Conway, SC. 17

Feb. 2000 <http://web7.infotrac.galegroup.com>.

How to Tell the Difference between a Scholarly Journal and a Popular Magazine

Scholarly journal articles tend to be relatively long, while popular magazine articles are rarely more than a few pages in length. If you are looking at a copy of the publication, scholarly journals tend to be rather plain looking with a great deal of text and few if any pictures or illustrations. They are written by experts with the expectation that the articles will be read by students or other scholars doing research or keeping up with the latest advancements in their fields of expertise. Scholarly journal articles often end with a list of works cited or consulted; a popular magazine article would be unlikely to include a bibliography. Popular magazines often have as many pictures and advertisements as pages of text and are written for general readers, not experts or scholars. Although some scholarly journals are published weekly or monthly, the majority are published four times per year (quarterly). Popular magazines tend to be published much more frequently than scholarly journals (weekly, biweekly, monthly, or bimonthly).

If you can find a copy of the periodical in your library, the front matter of any issue will tell you how frequently the journal or magazine is published, but bear in mind that some scholarly journals are published weekly, so frequency of publication does not always tell you whether you are citing a journal or a popular magazine.

Your library's periodicals list, which should be available on your library's Web site and in print form, will usually tell you whether you are looking at a magazine or journal article. For more information on the publication, search your library's online catalog under the title of the journal or magazine.

You can also check for information about a journal or magazine in a directory such as Standard Periodical Directory (Z6951/.S78) or Ulrich's International Periodicals Directory (Z6941/.U5).

If you are still not certain what type of publication you are citing, ask a librarian or your professor to help you.

A Scholarly Journal Article from EBSCOhost: MasterFILE Premier

Johnson, David. "You've Never Seen Anything Like It." Theatre
    Crafts International (TCI): The Business of Entertainment
    Technology and Design 32.10 (1998): 5 pp. Full-text.

EBSCOhost: MasterFILE Premier. Online. EBSCO Information
    Services. UNC Wilmington Library, Wilmington, NC. 20 Feb.
    2000 <http:ebsco.more.net>.

A Scholarly Journal Article from
EBSCOhost: Academic Search Elite

Schwab, Milinda. "A Watch for Emily." Studies in Short Fic-
    tion 28.2 (1991): 215-17. Full-text. EBSCOhost: Academic
    Search Elite. Online. EBSCO Information Services. Horry-
    Georgetown Technical College Library, Conway, SC. 13 Apr.
    2000 <http://ehostvgw14>.

A Scholarly Journal Article from
America: History and Life

Nelson, Michael C. "Writing during Wartime: Gender and Literacy
    in the American Civil War." Journal of American Studies
    [Great Britain] 31.1 (1997): 43-68. Abstract. America:
    History and Life. Online. ABC-CLIO. Kimbel Library, Con-
    way, SC. 10 Feb. 2000 <http://sb2.abc-clio.com>.

A Newspaper Article from
NewsBank NewsFile Collection

Hamilton, Arnold, and Rachel Boehm. "Andrew May Be Century's
    Most Destructive Storm." Dallas Morning News 30 Aug. 1992:
    A1. Full-text. NewsBank NewsFile Collection. Online.
    NewsBank. Kimbel Library, Conway, SC. 17 Feb. 2000
    <http://infoweb8.newsbank.com>.

A Weekly Magazine Article from SIRS Knowledge Source

Watson, Traci. "What Really Plumps You Up?" US News and World
    Report 12 Dec. 1994: 80-81. Full-text. SIRS Knowledge

Source. Online. SIRS. Kimbel Library, Conway, SC. 17 Feb.

2000 <http://sks.sirs.com>.

Citing Free Online Reference Databases

When you are citing materials taken from a free online database, follow the guidelines for citing an article from a subscription online database as described in the model citations discussed earlier in this chapter, but give the full electronic address of the article at the end of your citation, not just the URL for the home page of the database.

Note that ERIC is available as both a subscription database and as a free database in different versions. If you can access the database without going through a library Web page, the database is free for anyone to use. Many free databases such as ERIC are sponsored by the federal government. Check your library's Web page for a list of free reference databases.

A Scholarly Journal Article from ERIC

Baker, Nancy Westrich. "The Effect of Portfolio-Based In-

struction on Composition Students' Final Examination

Scores, Course Grades, and Attitudes toward Writing."

Research in the Teaching of English 27.2 (1993): 155-74.

Abstract. ERIC. Online. Educational Resources Informa-

tion Center Clearinghouse on Assessment and Evaluation

at U Maryland. 17 Feb. 2000 <http://ericae.net/ericdb/

EJ463729.htm>.

A Conference Paper Available from ERIC

Martin, Eric V. "More Than Just Assessing: A Discussion of

Questions, Concerns, and Complications Related to Port-

folio Evaluation." Conference on College Composition

and Communication. Phoenix, AZ. March 12-15. Abstract.

ERIC. Online. Educational Resources Information Center

Clearinghouse on Assessment and Evaluation at U Maryland.

3 Feb. 2000 <http://ericae.net/ericdb/ED414597.htm>.

Citing Online Encyclopedias and Dictionaries

An Entry from an Online Encyclopedia

"Dickinson, Emily Elizabeth." Encyclopaedia Britannica Online.

1998. Encyclopaedia Britannica. 21 Feb. 2000. <http://

members.eb.com/bol/topic?eu=30830&sctn=1&pm=1>.

"Onassis, Jacqueline Bouvier Kennedy." Grolier Multimedia

Encyclopedia. 2000. Grolier. 17 Feb. 2000 <http://

gme.grolier.com/cgi-bin/gme_bp?artbaseid=0214230>.

"Transcendentalism." Encyclopedia Americana Online. 2000.

Grolier. 17 Feb. 2000 <http://ea.grolier.com/cgi-bin/

build-page?artbaseid=0390540-00>.

1. Give the author of the entry (if known), last name first.
2. If no author is given, begin the entry with the title of the article in double quotation marks followed by a period inside the final quotation marks.
3. Give the title exactly as it appears in the encyclopedia (names inverted).
4. Give the title of the online encyclopedia (underlined).
5. Give the version number if available (e.g., Vers. 3.0.).
6. Give the date of publication, copyright, or most recent update.
7. Give the name of the publisher of the database.
8. Give the date you accessed the material.
9. Give the electronic address in angle brackets followed by a period.

A Photograph from an Online Encyclopedia

"Onassis, Jacqueline Kennedy." Photograph. Grolier Multi-

media Encyclopedia. 2000. Grolier. 17 Feb. 2000

<http://gme.grolier.com/cgi-bin/

gme_bp?artbaseid=0214230&assettype=p>.

A Definition from an Online Dictionary

"Deism." <u>Merriam-Webster Online</u>. 1999. Encyclopaedia Britan-

    nica. 21 Feb. 2000 <http://members.eb.com/cgi-bin/

    dictionary?va=Deism>.

1. Give the word in double quotation marks, followed by a period.
2. Give the title of the online dictionary (underlined).
3. Give the date of publication, copyright, or most recent update.
4. Give the name of the publisher of the dictionary (if available).
5. Give the date you accessed the definition.
6. Give the electronic address in angle brackets followed by a period.

Material Accessed through a Keyword or Path Search

"Frost, Robert." <u>Compton's Encyclopedia Online</u>. Vers. 3.0.

    1998. America Online. 3 May 2000. Keyword: Compton's.

If you found the material you are using by doing a keyword search on an Internet service such as America Online, type the word *Keyword* followed by a colon and one space and give the word you used to search for the information you are citing.

If you found the information you are citing by using a series of keywords to access information through a search engine, type the word *Path* followed by a colon and one space and give the path you followed to find the information using semicolons to separate the terms (e.g. Path: education; K-12; teaching; American literature; Robert Frost.)

CHAPTER 14

Parenthetical Citations

When you use an author's original interpretation or idea or an author's precise wording, you must inform your reader precisely where in your source (what page or pages) the material came from by using a parenthetical citation (also called a parenthetical reference). The parenthetical citation refers your reader to the complete information about that particular source given on your works-cited page.

- Most parenthetical citations contain the author's last name followed by the page number in the source (Thompson 34) or the page number alone (34) if the author's name has been incorporated into your sentence.
- If you are referring to the entire work rather than to a specific page in the work, you may give the author's name in your sentence and omit the parenthetical citation. (See example on page 35.)
- Omit from the parenthetical citation any information (such as the author's name or the title of the work) given in the introduction to your quotation, summary, or paraphrase.
- Check your works-cited list carefully to make sure you have provided complete information on all the sources in your parenthetical citations.

Author's Name Not Given in Your Sentence

Give the author's name followed by one space and the page number(s) from the source. Do not type a comma between the author's name and the page reference. Do not use the abbreviations *p.* and *pp.*

```
Pearl is "precociously intelligent" (McNamara 539).
```

Author's Name Given in Your Sentence

```
McNamara points out that Pearl is "precociously intelligent"
(539).
```

Author's Name Not Given in Source

Magazines and newspapers sometimes do not give the name of the author of an article, so give the title or a shortened version of the title beginning with the word by which the source was alphabetized in your works-cited list. You may give the section letter as well as the page number of a newspaper article, as illustrated in the next entry.

```
("Problems with Children" B4)
```

Quotation Taken from Two Consecutive Pages

If your quotation begins at the bottom of one page in your source and continues on the top of the next page, use inclusive page numbers.

```
"Pearl is pure symbol, the living emblem of the sin, a human

embodiment of the Scarlet Letter," writes Richard Harter Fogle

(312-13).
```

Two or More Works by the Same Author

To make sure your reader knows which of the works you are referring to, type a comma and one space after the author's name and give the title or a recognizable shortened form of the title beginning with the word by which the title was alphabetized in your list of works cited.

```
(Hawthorne, The Scarlet Letter 78) or (Hawthorne, Scarlet 78)

(Hawthorne, The Marble Faun 272) or (Hawthorne, Marble 272)
```

Two Authors Not Named in Your Sentence

```
(Hampton and Johnson 356)
```

Three Authors Not Named in Your Sentence

```
(Smith, Green, and Jones 458)
```

Four or More Authors Not Named in Your Sentence

Give the last name of the first author listed on the title page followed by *et al.* (Latin for "and others").

```
(Smithfield et al. 456)
```

Works by Two Authors with the Same Last Name

(J. Williams 456)

(G. Williams 897)

Works by Two Authors with the Same Initial and Last Name

(James Williams 27)

(Joseph Williams 38)

Citing Several Volumes of a Multivolume Work

If you quoted or paraphrased from only one volume of a multivolume work, give the volume you used in your works-cited list. However, if you quoted or paraphrased from two or more volumes of a multivolume work, type the author's name (if not given in your sentence); then type the volume number, a colon, one space, and the page numbers.

(Wilson 2: 456-57)

(Wilson 4: 243-44)

Citing Paragraphs, Screens, Grids, or Items

If you need to specify anything other than a page number, type a comma and one space after the author's name and either type the appropriate word or use the MLA-recommended abbreviation followed by the number(s). (See chapter 22 for a list of MLA-recommended abbreviations.)

(Franklin, par. 7)

(Franklin, pars. 8-9)

(Millworth, screens 4-5)

(Brown, grids 7-9)

(Jackson, item 78)

Citing Several Works

Use semicolons followed by one space to separate the citations. This information could also be given in a footnote or an endnote (also called a note), which is a much better choice if your parenthetical citation will be long. (See chapter 15 for more information on formatting footnotes and endnotes.)

```
(Smith 345; Green 248; Thompson 786)
```

A Quotation from a Literary Work

Give the reader enough information to locate the quotation in any edition of the work. After the page number from the edition you used, type a semicolon and use MLA-recommended abbreviations to specify the chapter (*ch.*), book (*bk.*), paragraph (*par.*), part (*pt.*), section (*sec.*), scene (*sc.*), and so on. (See chapter 22 for a list of MLA-recommended abbreviations.

```
Hawthorne describes Pearl as "the scarlet letter endowed with
life" (70; ch. 7).
```

A Quotation from a Short Poem

In your first parenthetical citation, type *line* or *lines* (lines 4–8). Once you have informed your reader that you are giving line numbers rather than page numbers, you may give the line numbers alone (4–8). Do not use the abbreviations *l.* or *ll.* because they can be confused with numbers.

A Quotation from a Long Poem

If a poem is long enough to be divided into books or cantos, type the title of the poem (underlined), the book or canto number, a period followed by no space, and the line or line numbers. The citation that follows refers to book 7, lines 24–28 of Homer's <u>Odyssey</u>.

```
(Odyssey 7.24-28)
```

A Quotation from a Shakespearean or Other Classic Verse Play

Underline the title of the play. Give the act, scene, and line numbers in Arabic numerals separated by periods.

```
(Hamlet 3.1.56-58)
```

A Quotation from the Bible

Give the name of the book, and then the chapter and verse in Arabic numerals separated by periods. Do not underline the titles of books of the Bible. You may abbreviate the names of books of the Bible: *Gen.* for Genesis, for example.

(Gen. 2.10)

An Online Source

If a Web site has page numbers or paragraph numbers, use them in your parenthetical citations. Many Web documents, however, are not paginated, nor do they have numbered paragraphs. For those documents, you do not have to give a page or paragraph number in your parenthetical citation; just name the author(s) either in your sentence or in the parenthetical citation at the end of your sentence (e.g., Brower). You may also use the MLA abbreviation *n. pag.* to assure your reader that no pages were given for you to cite (e.g., Brower n. pag.).

Some instructors will ask you to turn in photocopies of all print materials and printouts of Web materials cited in your paper. An instructor who is checking your citations for accuracy may need you to identify the pages in the Web site printouts from which you quoted, paraphrased, or summarized information. In this case, follow your instructor's guidelines for giving printout page numbers in your parenthetical citations. MLA allows you to give additional information beyond the minimum requirements if you think such information will be useful to your reader.

Quoting/Paraphrasing/Summarizing from an Indirect Source

If you are reading Robert T. Brown's book analyzing the novels of Thomas Hardy, Brown's words and ideas are your *original* source of information. If Brown quotes from Charles K. Smith to support a point he is making and you wish to quote Smith's words in your paper, you are using an *indirect* source. If your instructor has asked you not to use indirect sources in your paper, then you must find Charles K. Smith's article or book so that you can quote from the original source. If your instructor has no objections to your quoting from an indirect source, follow the guidelines discussed here.

Short Quotation (One to Four Lines)
Taken from an Indirect Source

1. The material you are quoting will be in double quotation marks in your source. Use double quotation marks around the quoted material to show that you are quoting and change the double quotation marks in your source to single quotation marks to show that the material was quoted in your source.
2. If you are quoting a brief passage from a long, block quotation in your source, you must enclose that material in both single quotation marks (to show that the material was quoted in the source rather than written by the author of the source) and double quotation marks (to show that you are quoting the material).

Long Quotation (Five or More Lines)
Taken from an Indirect Source

If the material you are quoting takes up five or more lines of space when typed into your paper, indent the quotation one inch (or ten spaces on a typewriter) from the left margin and enclose the block material in double quotation marks in your paper to show that it was quoted in your source.

Parenthetical Citations for Quotations
Taken from an Indirect Source

You will also need to identify both the writer of the words you are quoting and the author of the essay, article, or book from which you are quoting. If Robert T. Brown quoted Charles K. Smith in your source and you wish to use Smith's words, use one of the parenthetical citations that follow.

Smith named in your sentence:

(qtd. in Brown 346)

Smith not named in your sentence:

(Smith qtd. in Brown 346)

Smith paraphrased by Brown:

(Smith para. in Brown 346)

General Knowledge of a Subject: No Parenthetical Citation Needed

1. You need not give a parenthetical citation when you present general knowledge material in your own words.

2. For example, if you are writing a literary analysis, you may describe events that occur in the story, novel, play, or poem without a parenthetical citation as long as you do not use the author's precise wording.

3. Biographical information about a famous person can be found without a parenthetical citation, footnote, or endnote in many sources. Therefore, you may give general information about someone's life (where the person was born, where he or she was educated, whom he or she married, when he or she died, when a particular novel, story, poem, or play was published) without a parenthetical citation as long as you do not use the precise wording of your source.

4. If you see information discussed in several of your sources without being credited to other sources, you may safely assume that the information is general knowledge and need not be cited to a source in your paper.

5. Remember, however, that the precise wording of a source must always be cited to the person who wrote the words because not to do so is plagiarism. (See chapter 21 for more information about plagiarism.)

6. If you are not sure whether the information you are using is general knowledge, the best plan is to give a parenthetical citation rather than to risk being accused of plagiarizing from your sources.

Punctuating Parenthetical Citations: Short Quotations

Citation at the End of a Short Quotation

Place the parenthetical citation **before the period** that ends the sentence.

```
That Linda Loman truly loves her husband seems obvious when she

tells Biff and Happy, "He's just a big stupid man to you, but

I tell you there's more good in him than in many other people"

(Miller 1663).
```

Citation in the Middle of a Quoted Sentence

If the quotation appears in the first half of the sentence, place the parenthetical citation as close as possible to the quotation and **before any punctuation** that appears in the middle of the sentence.

```
Although, as Hawthorne tells us, "Pearl [. . .] could have

borne a fair examination in the New England Primer" (77; ch. 8),

she refuses to give the expected answer to Mr. Wilson's ques-

tion as to who created her.
```

Citation after a Question Mark or Exclamation Point

A question mark or exclamation point that ends a quotation should be typed inside the final quotation marks. Then type one space, the parenthetical citation, and a period to end the sentence.

```
As they make plans to run away together, Hester promises Arthur

that they can escape their shame: "'Let us not look back

[. . .]. The past is gone! Wherefore should we linger upon it

now?'" (Hawthorne 137; ch. 18).

Biff is so upset that he literally screams at his father,

"We never told the truth for ten minutes in this house!"

(Miller 1702).
```

Punctuating Parenthetical Citations: Long, Block Quotations

1. Place the parenthetical citation **after the period or other punctuation** that ends a block quotation.
2. Note that the double quotation marks used to punctuate the dialogue in the novel are used precisely as printed in the source in the block quotation that follows.
3. Note that the second paragraph in this quotation is indented an additional one quarter inch (on a computer) or an additional three spaces (on a typewriter) from the left margin to mark the change of paragraphs in the source.

4. The first line of the quotation is not indented an additional quarter inch (or three spaces) because it was not the first sentence in the paragraph in which it was printed in the novel. If the first line of the quotation had also been the first sentence in the paragraph in the novel, it would have been indented an additional one fourth inch (or three spaces) from the left margin.

Hawthorne makes it clear that Chillingworth's revenge is the worst sin in The Scarlet Letter:

> "We are not, Hester, the worst sinners in the world. There is one worse than even the polluted priest! That old man's revenge has been blacker than my sin. He has violated, in cold blood, the sanctity of a human heart. Thou and I, Hester, never did so!"
>
> "Never, never!" whispered she. "What we did had a consecration of its own. We felt it so! We said so to each other! Hast thou forgotten it?" (133; ch. 17)

CHAPTER 15

Endnotes and Footnotes

Endnotes and footnotes are used to give information that does not fit well into the text of your paper but may be of interest to your reader. Notes that give additional information are called **content notes.** Notes that list additional or indirect sources are called **bibliographic notes.** Endnotes are typed in a list at the end of the paper and footnotes are typed at the bottoms of the pages. You need not use endnotes or footnotes, but if you wish to give additional information, endnotes are easier to organize and are preferred by most instructors.

Notes can be used for the following purposes:

- To give additional information or further explanation
- To define a term your reader might not understand
- To comment on or evaluate a source
- To give the source of additional information
- To give the source of a contrasting interpretation
- To list multiple sources
- To give full publication information for an indirect source

[1] For a contrasting interpretation of Hamlet's state of mind in this scene, see Harrison 56-58.

[2] For a more complete discussion of Plath's relationship to Hughes, see Smith 89-94; Johnson 234-39; Brewer 95-105.

[3] Charles K. Smith, <u>Thomas Hardy: The Early Novels</u> (New York: Oxford UP, 1998) 276.

Endnotes

1. Center the word *Notes* one inch from the top of a new page, double-space, and begin your list of notes.
2. Double-space everything on your endnote page.
3. The first line of an endnote is indented one-half inch (on computer) or five spaces (on a typewriter) from the left margin; subsequent lines begin flush with the left margin.

Formatting Footnotes and Endnotes on a Computer

Most word-processing programs will format footnotes and endnotes for you. In Microsoft Word, you will find the footnote/endnote function under the "Insert" menu.

4. Type the endnote number on the top half of the line at the end of the sentence in your paper to which the note refers. This is called a superscript number.
5. Type the endnote number on the top half of the line at the beginning of the note on the endnote page. Leave one space between the endnote number and the material in the endnote.
6. Number the endnote page as a part of your text, and place it after the last page of your paper and before the list of works cited.

Footnotes

1. Footnotes are typed at the bottoms of the pages.
2. Leave four lines (two double spaces) between your text and the first footnote.
3. Single-space the material in each footnote, but double-space between the footnotes.
4. If you need to continue a footnote from one page to the next, double-space after the text for the next page ends, type a line across the page, and double-space again. Then begin the footnote continued from the previous page followed by the rest of the footnotes for that page.
5. Number footnotes consecutively throughout the paper.

CHAPTER 16

Quotations

> AVOID USING AN EXCESSIVE NUMBER OF QUOTATIONS IN YOUR PAPER. MOST OF THE PAPER SHOULD BE YOUR OWN EXPLANATION OR ANALYSIS OF THE SUBJECT PRESENTED IN YOUR OWN WORDS.

Use quotations for the following reasons:

- To vividly illustrate a point you want the reader to see
- To back up what you have said with an expert's opinion
- To prove to your reader that you have adequately researched your topic by incorporating expert opinions into your text
- Because the writer in your source has explained a point so precisely and beautifully that a paraphrase or summary would not do justice to the original

Sometimes using a quotation is much more vivid than explaining an idea in your own words.

Explanation of an idea in your own words:

```
Biff tells his father that they are both ordinary men--not
winners.
```

Quotation:

```
Biff tells his father, "Pop! I'm a dime a dozen, and so are
you!" (Miller 1703).
```

Your explanation combined with the author's vivid wording:

```
Biff tells his father that they are both ordinary men--not win-
ners: "Pop! I'm a dime a dozen, and so are you!" (Miller 1703).
```

Short Quotations

- One to four lines in length when the quoted material is typed into your paper.
- In double quotation marks within the regular text of the paper.
- Double-spaced.
- Not indented.
- Words or phrases that appear in double quotation marks in your source should be typed in single quotation marks in your text.
- Words underlined or printed in bold in your source should be underlined or formatted in bold in your paper.
- Because underlining is easier to notice than italics, follow the MLA recommendation to underline in your paper any material that appears in italics in your sources.
- An ellipsis (three spaced periods enclosed in square brackets) should be used to indicate that material that is not already obvious has been omitted from the quotation.
- The parenthetical citation should be placed at the end of the quotation and **before** the nearest internal or the final punctuation mark.
- Always connected to your text by an introduction or lead-in of some sort—naming the writer or speaker, if possible.

```
In the beginning moments of his short story "The Open Boat,"
Stephen Crane emphasizes the violence of the sea: "These waves
were most wrongfully and barbarously abrupt and tall, and each
froth-top was a problem in small boat navigation" (1536).
```

Long, Block Quotations

- Five or more lines in length when the quoted material is typed into your paper.
- Indented one inch (or ten spaces on a typewriter) from the left margin.
- Not indented from the right margin.
- Double-spaced.
- No quotation marks are necessary (unless they appear in the text you are quoting) because indenting the material identifies it as a quotation.
- Any single or double quotation marks should be copied exactly as they appear in your source.

- Any words underlined or printed in bold should be reproduced exactly as they appear in your source.
- Words printed in italics in your source should be underlined in your paper.
- An ellipsis (three spaced periods enclosed in square brackets) should be used to indicate that material that is not already obvious has been omitted from the quotation.
- The parenthetical citation should be placed at the end of the quotation and **after** the final punctuation mark.
- Always connected to your text with an introduction or lead-in of some sort—naming the writer or speaker, if possible.

Michael J. Colacurcio writes:

> So teasing do Hawthorne's connections and analogies come to seem, that we are eventually led to wonder whether <u>The Scarlet Letter</u> shows only this one set of historical footprints. If Hester Prynne bears relation to Ann Hutchinson, would it be too outrageous to look for similarities between Arthur Dimmesdale and John Cotton, that high Calvinist who was variously asserted and denied to be the [Hutchinson's] partner in heresy? And [. . .] might there not be some fundamental relation between the deepest philosophicel [sic] and theological "issues" raised by the Antinomian Controversy and the "themes" of Hawthorne's romance? (216)

1. In the preceding quotation, the writer's full name is given in the introduction to the quotation, rather than the last name at the end in the parenthetical citation. If you had cited material from this writer earlier in your paper, you would give only the last name in your introduction (e.g., Colacurcio writes:).

2. The italics used in the source to format the title of the novel (*The Scarlet Letter*) was changed to underlining in accordance with the MLA recommendation that underlining should be substituted for italics in material that will be graded or copyedited.

3. The word *the* is clarified by placing *Hutchinson's* in square brackets.

4. An ellipsis (three spaced periods in square brackets) is used to indicate that a phrase was omitted between the word *And* and the word *might*.

5. The Latin word *sic* in square brackets is used to show that the word *philosophical* was misspelled in the source and is not your typing error.

6. The double quotation marks around the words *issues* and *themes* are copied exactly as they appear in the original text of the quotation.

7. The parenthetical citation is placed **after** the punctuation mark ending the quoted material.

Indenting Paragraphs in a Block Quotation

1. If you are quoting two or more entire paragraphs from your source, indent the first sentence of each new paragraph you quote an additional one quarter inch (one and one quarter inches total) from the left margin if you are working on a computer. On a typewriter, indent each new paragraph in your quotation an additional three spaces (thirteen spaces total) from the left margin.

2. If the first sentence of your quotation is not the first sentence in a new paragraph in your source, however, do not indent it more than the usual one inch (or ten spaces on a typewriter) from the left margin. Indent only the first sentence of the second or third paragraphs the additional one quarter inch (or three spaces).

In this scene the correspondent realizes for perhaps the first time that if he drowns in the sea, nature will continue without interruption, not even taking notice of his absence:

> When it occurs to a man that nature does not regard him as important, and that she feels she would not maim the universe by disposing of him, he at first wishes to throw bricks at the temple, and he hates deeply the fact that there are no bricks and no temples. Any visible expression of nature would surely be pelleted with his jeers.
>
> Then, if there be no tangible thing to hoot, he feels, perhaps, the desire to confront a personification and indulge in pleas, bowed to one knee, and with hands supplicant, saying, "Yes, but I love myself."

> A high cold star on a winter's night is the word
> he feels that she says to him. Thereafter he know the
> pathos of his situation. (Crane 190)

1. Note that three full paragraphs are quoted from Stephen Crane's short story "The Open Boat."
2. Each paragraph is indented one and one quarter inches from the left margin.
3. No quotation marks are used at the beginning or at the end of the quotation because the block format identifies the material as a quotation.
4. Note that the double quotation marks from the source are duplicated exactly as they appear in Crane's text. (If this was a short quotation, you would change Crane's double quotation marks to single quotation marks.)
5. Note that the parenthetical citation is typed after the period that ends the quotation. (If this had been a short quotation, the citation would have been typed before, not after the period which ends the sentence.)

Quoting Dialogue from a Novel or Short Story: Short Quotations

Dialogue quoted from a novel or short story should be placed in both single and double quotation marks. The double quotation marks tell your reader that you are quoting material from your source, and the single quotation marks replace the double quotation marks that appeared in your source.

> In the forest scene Hawthorne describes Pearl's intuitive sense
> of what Dimmesdale must do to save his soul: " 'Doth he love
> us?' said Pearl, looking up with acute intelligence into her
> mother's face. 'Will he go back with us, hand in hand, we three
> together into the town?' " (144; ch. 18).

Quoting Dialogue from a Play: Short Quotations

Dialogue quoted from a play will usually be printed without quotation marks in your source. In a short quotation, use double quotation marks around dialogue in a play.

> In a desperate attempt to escape from what he perceives as a fu-
> tile pursuit of the American Dream, Biff pleads with his father:

Naming the Writer or Speaker in the Introduction to a Quotation

1. As a general rule, give the name of the writer of the words you are quoting in your introduction to the quotation rather than in the parenthetical citation.

2. If it seems appropriate, you can also include the writer's credentials in your lead-in to the quotation. Why should your reader believe the opinions expressed by this writer?

3. Avoid, however, pointing out what will already be obvious to your reader. For example, you need not tell the reader of a literary analysis essay that you are quoting literary critics. Just give the critic's name in your lead-in.

4. The first time you quote (or paraphrase or summarize) from a literary critic or other expert writer, give his or her full name in the introduction to the material you are quoting. Thereafter, you may give only the writer's last name in your introductory material.

5. When you quote dialogue in papers analyzing literary works, identify the character who is speaking in your introduction to the quotation.

"Will you let me go, for Christ sake? Will you take that phony dream and burn it before something happens?" (Miller 1703).

Quoting Dialogue from a Play: Long Quotations

1. If you wish to quote dialogue between two or more characters in a play, indent the material you are quoting one inch (or ten spaces on a typewriter) from the left margin.

2. Type each character's name in all capital letters followed by a period and one space. Then type the character's speech, indenting all lines after the first line in the speech one quarter inch (one and one quarter inches total) from the left margin on a computer and three additional spaces (thirteen spaces total) from the left margin on a typewriter.

3. Then indent one inch or ten spaces from the left margin and type the second character's name in all capital letters followed by a period, one space, and that character's speech.

4. Except for the character identifications, reproduce exactly as in your source any words underlined or printed in bold. Underline any words printed in italics. In the following quotation, note that the stage

directions, which appeared in italics in the text of the play, have been
underlined in the student's quotation.

Willy believes his brother Ben has achieved the American Dream

and is therefore "a great man":

       WILLY. No! Boys! Boys! (<u>Young Biff and Happy appear</u>.)

          Listen to this. This is your Uncle Ben, a great

          man! Tell my boys, Ben!

       BEN. Why, boys, when I was seventeen I walked into the

          jungle, and when I was twenty-one I walked out. (<u>He</u>

          <u>laughs</u>.) And by God I was rich.

       WILLY. (<u>to the boys</u>) You see what I been talking about?

          The greatest things can happen! (Miller 1657)

Quoting Poetry: Short Quotations

1. One to three lines of poetry may be incorporated into the text of your
   paper in quotation marks. Type a space, a slash, and another space between each line to identify the line breaks.
2. Type single quotation marks around any words, phrases, or sentences
   that appear in double quotation marks in your source. Reproduce any
   underlining or bold appearing in your source. Underline any words appearing in italics in your source.

I often think of these lines by Robert Frost when I consider

the choices that have led me to this point in my life: "Two

roads diverged in a wood, and I-- / I took the one less trav-

eled by, / And that has made all the difference" (18-20).

3. However, if you wish to place special emphasis on one to three lines
   of poetry, indent the lines one inch (or ten spaces on a typewriter) from
   the left margin and reproduce the lines exactly as they appeared in
   your source.

Quoting Poetry: Long Quotations

1. If you are quoting four or more lines of poetry, indent the lines one inch
   (or ten spaces on a typewriter) from the left margin and type the lines

exactly as they appear in your source except that the lines should be double-spaced.

2. Do not use quotation marks around the lines because indenting the poetry identifies the lines as quoted material.

3. If any quotation marks appear in the poetry, reproduce them as they appear in your source. Reproduce exactly any underlining or bold, but underline any words appearing in italics in your source.

```
I often think of these lines by Robert Frost when I consider
the choices that have led me to this point in my life:
        I shall be telling this with a sigh
        Somewhere ages and ages hence:
        Two roads diverged in a wood, and I--
        I took the one less traveled by,
        And that has made all the difference. (16-20)
```

4. If the lines you are quoting are too long to fit on a single line in your text, you may reduce the indentation from the left margin to less than one inch (or to fewer than ten spaces on a typewriter) if this reduction will allow the lines to fit. If this plan does not work, continue the line of poetry onto the next line and indent an additional one quarter inch (or three additional spaces on a typewriter) to show your reader that this material is still part of the same line.

```
Walt Whitman describes the horrors of the Civil War in these
lines from his poem "The Wound-Dresser":
        I dress the perforated shoulder, the foot with the
            bullet-wound,
        Cleanse the one with a gnawing and putrid gangrene, so
            sickening, so offensive,
        While the attendant stands behind aside me holding the
            tray and pail.
        I am faithful. I do not give out.
        The fractured thigh, the knee, the wound in the
            abdomen,
        These and more I dress with impassive hand, (yet deep
            in my breast a fire, a burning flame). (50-56)
```

5. If the lines of the poem are arranged in an unusual way in your source, reproduce the spatial arrangement of the lines as closely as you can, reducing the indentation to fewer than one inch (or ten spaces) if necessary.

```
In these lines, George Herbert describes God's power to help

the sinner overcome adversity:

                        With thee

                    Let me combine,

                And feel this day thy victory

            For if I imp my wing on thine,

        Affliction shall advance the flight in me. (16-20)
```

Parenthetical Citation for a Short Poetry Quotation

1. In your first parenthetical citation, type *line* or *lines* (lines 4–8). Once you have informed your reader that you are giving line numbers rather than page numbers, you may give the line numbers alone (4–8). Do not use the abbreviations *l.* and *ll.* because they could be confused with numbers.
2. Type the parenthetical citation **before** the period that ends the sentence.

```
I often think of these lines by Robert Frost when I consider

the choices that have led me to this point in my life: "Two

roads diverged in a wood, and I-- / I took the one less

traveled by, / And that has made all the difference" (lines

18-20).
```

Parenthetical Citation for a Long, Block Poetry Quotation

1. At the end of the quotation, type a period or other end punctuation, one space, and the parenthetical citation.
2. If you use an ellipsis to show that you omitted the final words in a poetic sentence, type the ellipsis in square brackets. Then type a period followed by one space and the parenthetical citation.

3. If the parenthetical citation will not fit on the last line, type it on the
   next line so that it ends at the right margin.

```
Frost's poem "Mending Wall" begins with these lines:

        Something there is that doesn't love a wall,

        That sends the frozen-ground-swell under it

        And spills the upper boulders in the sun,

        And makes gaps even two can pass abreast.

        The work of hunters is another thing:

        I have come after them and made repair

        Where they have left not one stone on a stone [. . .].

                                           (lines 1-7)
```

4. Note that in the preceding quotation, the ellipsis in square brackets
   shows that the word *stone* is not the last word in the poetic sentence.
   (In the source, a comma appears after the word *stone,* not a period.)
5. Note that because the parenthetical citation would not fit on the last
   line quoted, it is typed so that it ends flush with the right margin.

Using an Ellipsis to Omit Lines of Poetry

1. If you wish to omit one or more lines from a block poetic quotation,
   type a line of spaced periods inside square brackets.
2. Note that in the quotation that follows, double quotation marks are reproduced exactly as they appeared in the source—except that because
   the word *cows* was not the last word in the quoted material in the
   poem, a double quotation mark was supplied to indicate that the material between the italicized word *Why* and the word *cows* was punctuated as dialogue in the poem.
3. Note that the word *Why,* which was in italics in the source, is underlined in the quotation.

```
The contrast between the speaker and his neighbor is obvious in

these lines by Robert Frost:

        Spring is the mischief in me, and I wonder

        If I could put a notion in his head:
```

"<u>Why</u> do they make good neighbors? Isn't it

Where there are cows? But here there are no cows."

[. . . . .]

He moves in darkness as it seems to me,

Not of woods only and the shade of trees.

                                              (28-31, 41-42)

CHAPTER 17

Using Square Brackets in Quotations

Because you must quote precisely, any changes you make to a quotation must be placed in square brackets. If square brackets are not available on your keyboard, leave spaces and add them with a pen.

Use Brackets to Explain Something That Might Be Unclear to Your Reader or to Give Additional Information

```
Although, as Hawthorne tells us, "Pearl [. . .] could have
borne a fair examination in the New England Primer [a popular
textbook that taught religious precepts to the Puritan chil-
dren] " (77; ch. 8), she refuses to give the expected answer to
Mr. Wilson's question as to who created her.
```

The bracketed explanation identifying the New England Primer could also be placed in a footnote or endnote, which is a better choice if the explanatory material is lengthy.

Use Brackets to Clarify a Pronoun

If the noun to which a pronoun in your quotation refers (the antecedent of the pronoun) might be unclear to your reader, identify the noun in square brackets after the pronoun or replace the unclear pronoun with the noun in square brackets.

```
Hawthorne writes, "Tempted by a dream of happiness, he [Dimmes-
dale] had yielded himself with deliberate choice, as he had
never done before, to what he knew was deadly sin" (150; ch. 18).
```

Use Brackets to Change Verb Tenses

It is common practice to analyze literary works in present tense. Thus you would write, "Pearl **is** a difficult child" rather than "Pearl **was** a difficult child" in an analysis of Hawthorne's The Scarlet Letter. If you are quoting a critic who has used a past tense verb in a particular sentence, you may change the tense of the critic's verb by typing the tense you wish to use in square brackets. This bracketed change of tense avoids an awkward verb tense shift in your text.

As a general rule of thumb, however, avoid changing the tense of verbs in the text of a literary work you are analyzing. One way to avoid the need to change tenses in brackets is to quote short phrases from the source rather than entire sentences.

Original sentence containing an awkward verb tense shift:

As Frederick C. Crews points out, "Hawthorne carried symbolism to the border of allegory but did not cross over" (369).

Verb tense changed in brackets to avoid verb tense shift:

As Frederick C. Crews points out, "Hawthorne [carries] symbolism to the border of allegory but [does] not cross over" (369).

Short phrases quoted to avoid the need for a bracketed tense change:

Frederick C. Crews points out that although Hawthorne often takes his symbolism "to the border of allegory," he does not "cross over" (369).

Use Brackets to Change a Capital Letter to a Lowercase Letter

Sometimes when you are quoting, your sentence structure requires a lowercase letter rather than a capital letter or vice versa. You may change the letter in square brackets.

When Hawthorne tells us that "[t]he scarlet letter had not done its office" (114; ch. 13), he means that Hester has not yet learned the lesson the scarlet letter was intended to teach her.

Use Brackets to Change a Lowercase Letter to a Capital Letter

Hawthorne describes Hester's acceptance of the pain inflicted upon her by the scarlet letter in this scene:

```
[L]ittle Pearl paused to gather the prickly burrs

from a tall burdock, which grew beside the tomb. Tak-

ing a handful of these, she arranged them along the

lines of the scarlet letter that decorated the mater-

nal bosom, to which the burrs, as their nature was,

tenaciously adhered. Hester did not pluck them off.

(92; ch. 10)
```

Note that no ellipsis is needed before the word *[L]ittle* because the bracketed letter informs the reader that the material preceding the bracketed letter was omitted.

Using [sic] to Indicate an Error in Your Source

You must quote precisely from your sources. Therefore, if you find a logical, typographical, spelling, grammatical, punctuation, or other type of error in the material you wish to quote, do not correct it. Instead, type the word *sic* (Latin for "thus") in square brackets after the error to show your reader that the error was in your source and is not your copying or typing error.

Note that in the quotation that follows, the word *religious* was misspelled in the source. The error is identified as a typographical error in the source by the placement of [sic] after the misspelled word.

```
Hawthorne tells us that had it not been for her sin, Hester

"might have come down to us in history, hand in hand with Ann

Hutchinson, as the foundress of a religous [sic] sect" (113;

ch. 13).
```

Do Not Use [sic] after Intentional Errors Such as Dialect Spellings

```
In the last lines of the novel Huck tells us, "[T]here ain't

nothing more to write about, and I am rotten glad of it, be-

cause if I'd a knowed what a trouble it was to make a book I

wouldn't a tackled it and ain't a going to no more" (Twain

1418; ch. 43).
```

CHAPTER 18

Using an Ellipsis to Omit Words

If you wish to omit words, phrases, or sentences from a quotation that appears to be a complete sentence or paragraph, you must inform your reader that you have omitted material by using an ellipsis (three spaced periods in square brackets). The square brackets tell your reader that the omission is yours and that the spaced periods did not appear in your source.

1. You may not change the meaning the author intended by using an ellipsis.
2. Type one space before and after the ellipsis. Type one space before the second period and one space before the third period of the ellipsis. Leave no spaces before the first period or after the last period of the ellipsis: [. . .]
3. If the ellipsis falls at the end of your sentence, type one space before the ellipsis, but type the period and quotation mark immediately after the bracket that ends the ellipsis: [. . .]."
4. If a parenthetical citation is needed, type the quotation mark immediately after the bracket that ends the ellipsis: [. . .]" (312).

Read the following analysis of Pearl, the daughter of Hester Prynne, Nathaniel Hawthorne's most famous heroine, carefully so you will understand the examples that follow.

Original material from Richard Harter Fogle's book:

> Pearl is pure symbol, the living emblem of the sin, a human embodiment of the Scarlet Letter. Her mission is to keep Hester's adultery always before her eyes, to prevent her from attempting to escape its moral consequences. Pearl's childish questions are fiendishly apt; in speech and in action she never strays from the control of her symbolic function; her dress and her looks are related to the letter. When Hester casts the letter away in the forest, Pearl forces her to reassume it by flying into an uncontrollable rage. Yet despite the undeviating

```
arrangement of every circumstance which surrounds

her, no single action of hers is ever incredible

or inconsistent with the conceivable actions of any

child under the same conditions. (312-13)
```

No Ellipsis Is Needed with Quoted Phrases

You do not need to use an ellipsis or ellipses when you are quoting brief phrases from your source. The lowercase letters and incomplete sentence structures will make it clear to your reader that you have not quoted the entire sentence from your source.

```
As Richard Harter Fogle points out, Hawthorne uses Pearl as "a

human embodiment of the Scarlet Letter" (313).
```

Omitting Words from the Beginning of a Quoted Sentence

When you omit material from your source, be careful not to create an unclear sentence, a grammatically incorrect sentence, or a sentence fragment. Note that in the quotation that follows, the quoted material is a grammatically correct sentence even though some of it has been omitted.

The lowercase letter at the beginning of the quotation informs your reader that material has been omitted from the beginning of the sentence. Because the omission is obvious, no ellipsis is needed.

```
Richard Harter Fogle explains that "in speech and action [Pearl]

never strays from the control of her symbolic function; her

dress and her looks are related to the [scarlet] letter" (313).
```

In the next example, the lowercase letter that appears in Fogle's sentence is changed to a capital letter inside square brackets because the quoted material is a grammatically complete sentence, which must begin with a capital letter. The bracketed letter informs your reader that material has been omitted from the beginning of the sentence. Therefore, no ellipsis is needed.

```
According to Richard Harter Fogle, "[I]n speech and action

[Pearl] never strays from the control of her symbolic function;

her dress and her looks are related to the [scarlet] letter"

(313).
```

Ellipsis Used to Omit Words in the Middle of a Sentence

Note that even with the omission, the following quotation is a clear, grammatically correct sentence.

"Pearl is pure symbol, [. . .] a human embodiment of the Scarlet Letter," writes Richard Harter Fogle (312-13).

Ellipsis Used to Omit Words at the End of a Sentence

"Pearl is pure symbol, the living emblem of the sin, a human embodiment of the Scarlet Letter. Her mission is to keep Hester's adultery always before her eyes [. . .]," writes Richard Harter Fogle (312-13).

Ellipsis Used to Omit a Sentence or Several Sentences from a Block Quotation

After the end period, type a space, the ellipsis (three spaced periods in square brackets), and another space. Then begin the next sentence you wish to quote.

Richard Harter Fogle writes:

> Pearl is pure symbol, the living emblem of the sin, a human embodiment of the Scarlet Letter. Her mission is to keep Hester's adultery always before her eyes, to prevent her from attempting to escape its moral consequences. [. . .] When Hester casts the letter away in the forest, Pearl forces her to reassume it by flying into an uncontrollable rage.
> (312-13)

Ellipsis Used to Omit Material from the Middle of One Sentence to the End of Another

Richard Harter Fogle explains that

> Pearl is pure symbol, the living emblem of the sin, a human embodiment of the Scarlet Letter. Her mission

is to keep Hester's adultery always before her eyes
[. . .]. When Hester casts the letter away in the
forest, Pearl forces her to reassume it by flying into an uncontrollable rage. Yet despite the
undeviating arrangement of every circumstance which
surrounds her, no single action of hers is ever
incredible or inconsistent with the conceivable
actions of any child under the same conditions.
(312-13)

Ellipsis Used to Show Material Omitted from the Middle of One Sentence to the Middle of Another Sentence

According to Richard Harter Fogle,

Pearl is pure symbol, the living emblem of the sin,
a human embodiment of the Scarlet Letter. Her mission is to keep Hester's adultery always before her
eyes, to prevent her from attempting to escape its
moral consequences. Pearl's childish questions are
fiendishly apt; [. . .] no single action of hers
is ever incredible or inconsistent with the conceivable actions of any child under the same conditions.
(312-13)

CHAPTER 19

Punctuating Quotations

When you quote, reproduce the internal punctuation of the original material exactly, except that in a short quotation, you may change double quotation marks in your source to single quotation marks to show that the material appeared in double quotation marks in your source. You may also alter the internal and end punctuation of a quotation so that the combination of the quoted material and your words is punctuated correctly.

Your lead-in or explanatory material combined with the quoted material must read as a correctly punctuated, grammatically correct sentence.

Using Single Quotation Marks inside Double Quotation Marks

In a short quotation, use single quotation marks inside double quotation marks to indicate that the material was already in quotation marks in the text from which you are quoting.

```
" 'If we don't all get ashore--' said the captain. 'If we don't
all get ashore, I suppose you fellows know where to send news
of my finish?' " (Crane 1541).
```

Altering End Punctuation

You may alter the end punctuation of a quotation so that the combination of the quoted material and your words is punctuated correctly.

Sentence as printed in Hawthorne's "Young Goodman Brown":

```
A stern, a sad, a darkly meditative, a distrustful, if not a
desperate man did he become from the night of that fearful
dream. (347)
```

Quotation incorporated into your paper (internal punctuation remains the same; end period changes to comma):

```
"A stern, a sad, a darkly meditative, a distrustful, if not a
desperate man did he become from the night of that fearful
dream," writes Hawthorne (347).
```

Using Commas, Periods, and Ending Quotation Marks

Commas and periods are always typed inside ending quotation marks.

```
"I enjoyed the book I read last night," she said.
She said, "I enjoyed the book I read last night."
```

A comma or period should be typed inside the single quotation mark when single and double quotation marks are used together.

```
"I enjoyed reading Poe's 'Annabel Lee,'" she said.
She said, "I enjoyed reading Poe's 'Annabel Lee.'"
```

Using Semicolons, Colons, and Ending Quotation Marks

Semicolons and colons are always typed outside ending quotation marks.

```
He asked if I had read Poe's "Annabel Lee"; I told him that I
had memorized it when I was a child.
```

Using Question Marks, Exclamation Points and Ending Quotation Marks

Question marks and exclamation points are typed inside the ending quotation marks when the quoted material is a question or exclamation.

```
"Did you read the story I told you about?" he asked.
```

A question mark or exclamation point is typed inside both the single and the double quotation marks when both are used.

```
The captain called to the correspondent, "'Come to the boat!
Come to the boat!'" (Crane 1551).
```

Question marks and exclamation points are typed outside the final quotation marks when your sentence is a question or exclamation but the quoted material is not.

```
Are you sure he said, "I'm going to the movies"?
```

If both your sentence and the quoted material are questions or exclamations, place the question mark or exclamation point inside the final quotation marks if they fall at the end of the sentence. Do not use two question marks or exclamation points.

```
Are you sure he asked, "Do you think she would go out with me?"
```

Punctuating Quotation Lead-Ins

When you place your author/speaker identification or other type of explanatory lead-in at the beginning of a quotation, you might think of your quotation as the meat in a sandwich. The quotation (the meat) is sandwiched between two slices of bread—the lead-in to the quotation and the parenthetical citation, which refers your reader to the complete information about your source presented in your works-cited list.

Although the lead-in is most often placed at the beginning of a quotation, the author/speaker identification or explanatory information about a quotation may, for variation, be placed at the middle or end of your quotation. This explanatory information connects your quotation to your text by identifying the writer or speaker of the words you are quoting or by explaining how the quotation relates to the point you are trying to explain by using the quotation.

An Author/Speaker Identification Lead-In with a Comma

```
Hawthorne explains, "Now Pearl knew well enough who made her
[. . .]" (77; ch. 8).
```

A Lead-In Ending in the Word *That*

When your lead-in ends in the word *that,* you do not need a comma before the quotation.

```
Hawthorne tells us that "[. . .] Pearl knew well enough who
made her [. . .]" (77; ch. 8), because her mother had taught
her about the Puritan beliefs.
```

Author Identification in the Middle of the Quotation

When you position your author/speaker identification or explanatory material in the middle of the quotation, set it off with commas.

"With sudden and desperate tenderness," writes Hawthorne, "she threw her arms around him, and pressed his head against her bosom; little caring though his cheek rested on the scarlet letter" (132; ch. 17).

Author Identification between Two Complete Sentences from Your Source

Use a semicolon between the two grammatically complete sentences to avoid a comma splice when your author/speaker identification or explanatory material falls between the two sentences.

"The tendency of her fate and fortunes had been to set her free," writes Hawthorne; "[t]he scarlet letter was her passport into regions where other women dared not tread" (136; ch 18).

Speaker Identification between Two Dialogue Sentences

To avoid a comma splice, use a semicolon after the speaker identification.

"'Preach! Write! Act!'" Hester tells her beloved Arthur; "'[d]o anything, save to lie down and die!'" (135; ch. 17).

A Full-Sentence Lead-In Ending with a Colon

Use a colon after a full sentence lead-in to a quotation.

Hawthorne describes Hester's all too brief moment of freedom from the scarlet letter in the forest scene: "So speaking, she undid the clasp that fastened the scarlet letter, and, taking it from her bosom, threw it to a distance among the withered leaves" (137; ch. 18).

CHAPTER 20

Paraphrasing and Summarizing

Paraphrasing

To paraphrase means to express in your own words the idea of another person. When you paraphrase, you replicate the idea of the writer in your source without using any characteristic wording from your source. If you need to use some of the original phrases from your source, simply place them in quotation marks. A good rule of thumb when paraphrasing is not to use any three words in the same order as found in your source.

Even though you are expressing the idea in your own words, you must inform your reader that you took the idea from a source

1. By identifying the writer at the beginning of your sentence so that your reader will know that the idea being expressed is not your own
2. By placing a parenthetical citation after the paraphrased material and inside the final punctuation mark of the sentence

Original sentence written by John Caldwell Stubbs:

Seeing himself as an aging husband who wronged Hester by bringing her to a loveless marriage, he can forgive her adultery as no more than a counter-balancing wrong. (385)

Direct Quotation (Precise Wording of Critic)

John Caldwell Stubbs writes, "Seeing himself as an aging husband who wronged Hester by bringing her to a loveless marriage, he [Chillingworth] can forgive her adultery as no more than a counter-balancing wrong" (385).

Paraphrase of Critic's Interpretation

John Caldwell Stubbs points out that Chillingworth is able to forgive Hester's adultery because he realizes that he has also wronged her by enticing her into marrying him--a much older man she has never loved (385).

Summarizing

To summarize is to present in your own words a shortened version (one or several sentences) of one or more paragraphs from your source

1. By identifying the writer at the beginning of your summary so that your reader will know that the ideas being expressed are not your own
2. By placing a parenthetical reference after the summarized material and inside the final punctuation mark of the final sentence of the summary

Original paragraph written by John Caldwell Stubbs:

In precisely this context are Hester and Chillingworth presented to us. They are part of the series of opposed images. Hester is almost literally an intensification of the young wife. She carries her child in her arms. The striking richness of her attire and her dark hair make her woman on the large scale. Hawthorne likens her to the madonna of Renaissance art. Her role as representative of unrestricted, natural emotions is made all the more clear by contrast with the beadle marching before her as an embodiment of "the whole dismal severity of the Puritan code of law." The role of the beadle is quickly subsumed by Chillingworth. Seeing himself as an aging husband who wronged Hester by bringing her to a loveless marriage, he can forgive her adultery as no more than a counter-balancing wrong. But he burns to make the escaped lover suffer. Here he becomes Hester's ultimate adversary. In his demoniacal drive, he embodies the severest aspects of the hard justice of the Puritans to which Hester stands irrevocably opposed. (385)

Summary of Critical Interpretation

```
John Caldwell Stubbs points out that Hawthorne sets up a sym-
bolic opposition between Hester and her wronged husband, Roger
Chillingworth. Whereas Hester represents the sort of person who
always follows the intuitive dictates of her heart, Roger rep-
resents the harsh Puritan justice that attempts to dictate the
path one must follow (385).
```

Summary Using Some of the Critic's Memorable Phrases

```
John Caldwell Stubbs points out that Hawthorne sets up a sym-
bolic opposition between Hester and her wronged husband, Roger
Chillingworth. Whereas Hester is "representative of unre-
stricted, natural emotions," Roger "embodies the severest as-
pects of the hard justice of the Puritans" (385).
```

Choosing What to Paraphrase or Summarize

If you are writing a literary analysis, you will find that the critics you are reading will summarize events that occurred in the plot prior to analyzing the meaning of those events. You should avoid paraphrasing or summarizing these ideas because you can describe events from the plot in your own words without parenthetical citations. What happens in the story, novel, or play is considered general knowledge about your subject because anyone who reads the work will know what happened in the plot.

Paraphrase or summarize the critic's interpretation of the meaning of the work he or she is analyzing, not the supportive illustrations and plot summaries.

Poor Choice of Material to Paraphrase

```
Robert Thomas points out that Willy Loman commits suicide at
the end of Death of a Salesman (85).
```

Anyone who has read <u>Death of a Salesman</u> knows that Willy Loman commits suicide at the end of the play. You can explain this without referring to a critic or using a parenthetical citation.

Better Choice of Material to Paraphrase

```
Robert Thomas believes that Willy's suicide at the end of the
play is a misguided act of love for his family (85).
```

Here the critic is expressing an interpretation of Willy's motivation in committing suicide, so this is a better choice of material to paraphrase.

CHAPTER 21

Avoiding Plagiarism

When you take **original ideas, opinions, or interpretations** or **an author's precise wording** from a source, you must let your reader know whose idea or wording you are using by giving a parenthetical citation and by citing the complete information about your source in the list of works cited located at the end of your paper.

Not to distinguish your ideas and wording from those of your sources is plagiarism. If even one sentence in your paper is plagiarized, your instructor must conclude that every other sentence in your paper may be plagiarized. Therefore, your paper is unacceptable and may earn a failing grade. Because plagiarism is considered cheating, you may also earn a failing grade in the course and be in violation of your school's honor code. The only way to avoid plagiarizing is to be absolutely certain you credit your sources properly when you use the precise wording of your sources and ideas or interpretations not your own and not general knowledge.

Original sentence written by John Caldwell Stubbs:

Seeing himself as an aging husband who wronged Hester by bringing her to a loveless marriage, he can forgive her adultery as no more than a counter-balancing wrong. (385)

Plagiarized sentence (plagiarized [stolen] phrases appear in blue):

Chillingworth sees himself as an aging husband who sinned against Hester by bringing her to a loveless marriage.

This sentence is plagiarized because

1. No quotation marks identify the phrases taken from the source; therefore, the writer is leading the reader to believe that the idea expressed and the wording of this sentence are original rather than borrowed from a source
2. The critic's name is not given in the introduction to the sentence
3. No parenthetical reference identifies the critic or the page on which those phrases appeared in the source

Plagiarized sentence (plagiarized phrases appear in blue):

```
John Caldwell Stubbs points out that Chillingworth sees himself
as an aging husband who sinned against Hester by bringing her
to a loveless marriage (385).
```

This sentence is also plagiarized because although the critic's name and the page number of the source are given, the precise words of the critic have been used without quotation marks to distinguish those words from the student's own words. The student is leading the reader to believe that he is paraphrasing when in reality he is stealing the critic's copyrighted phrases.

Plagiarizing Papers from the Internet

You might be tempted to download and turn in as your own one of the student papers you find on the Internet. To do so would be a violation not only of your personal sense of honor, but also of your school's honor code. Turning in someone else's work as your own is cheating. Even turning in a paper that you wrote for another class without asking the professor for permission to do so is considered cheating at most universities. If you are caught plagiarizing in any of these ways, you will almost certainly earn a failing grade on the paper and, most likely, a failing grade in the course as well. If you are found guilty of violating your school's honor code, you could be expelled.

You should be aware that your professor has access to a number of Web sites, such as <www.plagiarism.org>, that specialize in detecting plagiarism in student papers. Don't risk your reputation as an honest person. Do your own work, and be conscientious about crediting any sources from which you borrowed materials. When in doubt, give a citation. It's better to be safe than sorry.

CHAPTER 22

MLA-Recommended Abbreviations

In your works-cited or works-consulted list, you should abbreviate the names of states, Canadian provinces, countries, and time designations such as the names of days and all months with the exception of May, June, and July. In addition, you should abbreviate other terms as listed here. Be sure to use standard MLA-recommended abbreviations. It is acceptable, however, to write out in full any term you believe your reader may not understand.

- Omit periods and spaces in abbreviations consisting of all capital letters (*CD, LP, DVD, VCR, SC, NC, USA, USSR, AD, BC*).
- When you abbreviate one or two words by using all lowercase letters or a combination of capital and lowercase letters, end the abbreviations with periods (*abbr., bk., Scot., Swed., So. Amer., No. Amer., Gt. Brit.*).
- If each lowercase letter stands for a different word in a series of words, type a period after each letter, but not a space (*a.m., p.m., n.p., n.d., i.e.*). Note, however, that MLA does leave a space in the abbreviation meaning "no pagination" (*n. pag.*).

  Notable exceptions to this rule are abbreviations found in your dictionary such as *rpm* for "revolutions per minute" and *mph* meaning "miles per hour."
- Leave one space after any period that follows the initial in a person's name (E. E. Cummings, not E.E. Cummings; T. S. Eliot, not T.S. Eliot).
- In a parenthetical or bibliographical citation, an abbreviation that follows a period is always capitalized. Abbreviations that do not follow periods begin with lowercase letters.

Abr. ed.	Abridged edition
AD	*anno domini*; in the year of the Lord (as in "AD 1015")
a.m.	before noon (Latin: *ante meridiem*)
art.	article
arts.	articles
BC	Before Christ (as in "350 BC")
bk.	book
CD-ROM	compact disc read-only memory

cf.	compare
ch.	chapter
chs.	chapters
comp.	compiler
Comp.	Compiled by
dir.	director
Dir.	Directed by
Diss.	Dissertation
ed.	editor, edition
eds.	editors
Ed.	Edited by

2nd ed.	second edition		PhD	Doctor of Philosophy	
3rd ed.	third edition		p.m.	after noon (Latin: *post meridiem*)	
4th ed.	fourth edition				
e.g.	for example (Latin: *exempli gratia*)		proc.	proceedings	
			prod.	producer	
et al.	and others (Latin: *et alii* or *et aliae*)		Prod.	Produced by	
			pt.	part	
Fwd. by	forwarded by		qtd.	quoted	
i.e.	that is (Latin: *id est*)		Rev. ed.	Revised edition	
introd.	introduction		Rev. of	Review of	
ms.	manuscript		Rpt. in	Reprinted in	
mss.	manuscripts		sec.	section	
narr.	narrator		ser.	series	
Narr.	Narrated by		sess.	session	
n.d.	no date of publication		sic	thus; error in source	
N.p.	no city (place) of publication given		st.	stanza	
			trans.	translator	
n.p.	no publisher given		Trans.	Translated by	
n. pag.	no pages (pagination) given		U	University	
ns	new series of a journal		UP	University Press	
os	old or original series of a journal		URL	uniform resource locator; Web site address	
P	Press		Vol.	volume	
p.	page		vols.	volumes	
pp.	pages		vs.	versus; against	
par.	paragraph		v.	versus; against; preferred form for citing legal cases	
pars.	paragraphs				
perf.	performer		Writ.	Written by	
Perf.	Performed by				

Abbreviating Months

Write out the names of months within the text of your paper, but abbreviate the names of all months with the exception of May, June, and July in your works-cited or works-consulted list.

Jan.	January	May	May	Sept.	September
Feb.	February	June	June	Oct.	October
Mar.	March	July	July	Nov.	November
Apr.	April	Aug.	August	Dec.	December

Abbreviating States

Do not abbreviate the names of states in the text of your paper, but use the postal abbreviation for the name of a state used in a bibliographical citation, in a postal address, and in parentheses.

AK	Alaska	MT	Montana
AL	Alabama	NC	North Carolina
AR	Arkansas	ND	North Dakota
AZ	Arizona	NE	Nebraska
CA	California	NH	New Hampshire
CO	Colorado	NJ	New Jersey
CT	Connecticut	NM	New Mexico
DC	District of Columbia	NV	Nevada
DE	Delaware	NY	New York
FL	Florida	OH	Ohio
GA	Georgia	OK	Oklahoma
HI	Hawaii	OR	Oregon
IA	Iowa	PA	Pennsylvania
ID	Idaho	RI	Rhode Island
IL	Illinois	SC	South Carolina
IN	Indiana	SD	South Dakota
KS	Kansas	TN	Tennessee
KY	Kentucky	TX	Texas
LA	Louisiana	UT	Utah
MA	Massachusetts	VA	Virginia
MD	Maryland	VT	Vermont
ME	Maine	WA	Washington
MI	Michigan	WI	Wisconsin
MN	Minnesota	WV	West Virginia
MO	Missouri	WY	Wyoming
MS	Mississippi		

Abbreviating Provinces of Canada

Abbreviate the names of provinces of Canada in bibliographic citations. Do not abbreviate the names of Canadian provinces in the text of your paper except in a postal address or in parentheses.

AB	Alberta	ON	Ontario
BC	British Columbia	PE	Prince Edward Island
MB	Manitoba	PQ	Quebec (Province de Québec)
NB	New Brunswick	SK	Saskatchewan
NF	Newfoundland	YT	Yukon Territory
NS	Nova Scotia		

Abbreviating the Names of Countries and Continents

Give the full name of a country or continent when you mention it in a sentence in your paper. You may abbreviate the name of a country in documentation, in a postal address, or in parentheses. You may abbreviate USSR in all situations.

Afr.	Africa	Jap.	Japan
Alb.	Albania	Leb.	Lebanon
Ant.	Antarctica	Mex.	Mexico
Arg.	Argentina	Neth.	Netherlands
Arm.	Armenia	No. Amer.	North America
Aus.	Austria	Norw.	Norway
Austral.	Australia	NZ	New Zealand
Belg.	Belgium	Pan.	Panama
Braz.	Brazil	Pol.	Poland
Bulg.	Bulgaria	Port.	Portugal
Can.	Canada	PR	Puerto Rico
Den.	Denmark	PRC	People's Republic of China
Ecua.	Ecuador	Russ.	Russia
Eng.	England	Scot.	Scotland
Eur.	Europe	So. Amer.	South America
Fr.	France	Sp.	Spain
Ger.	Germany	Swed.	Sweden
Gr.	Greece	Switz.	Switzerland
Gt. Brit.	Great Britain	Turk.	Turkey
Hung.	Hungary	UK	United Kingdom
Ire.	Ireland	US	United States
Isr.	Israel	USA	United States of America
It.	Italy	USSR	Union of Soviet Socialist Republics

CHAPTER 23

Shortening the Names of Publishers

1. Shorten the names of well-known publishers (e.g., *Harcourt* for *Harcourt College Publishers*).

2. If a well-known publisher's name includes a person's name and initials, shorten it to the last name (e.g., *Knopf* for *Alfred A. Knopf, Inc.*; *Norton* for *W. W. Norton and Co., Inc.*)

3. Omit abbreviations such as *Co.* for *company* or *Inc.* for *incorporated*.

4. For less well-known publishers, you may give a more complete name (e.g., *Public Citizen Health Group* rather than *Public*; *Health Communications* rather than *Health*).

5. If you are not certain your reader will recognize a publisher's name when shortened, give the name in full or write out any part of the name that might cause confusion. For example, if you shortened *Friends United Press* to *Friends UP*, your reader might assume the publisher was Friends University Press. For this entry, use *Friends United P.*

6. If you are not certain your reader will recognize the acronym for a publisher's name (*SIRS* for *Social Issues Resources Series, Inc.*; *MLA* for *Modern Language Association of America*; *GPO* for *Government Printing Office*), give the publisher's name in full or use a more recognizable abbreviation (e.g., *Mod. Lang. Asso.* instead of *MLA*).

Addison	Addison Wesley Longman, Inc.
Allyn	Allyn and Bacon, Inc.
Basic	Basic Books
Cambridge UP	Cambridge University Press
Da Capo	Da Capo Press
Duke UP	Duke University Press
ERIC	Educational Resources Information Center
Farrar	Farrar, Straus and Giroux, Inc.
Gale	Gale Research, Inc.
GPO	Government Printing Office
Harcourt	Harcourt College Publishers
Harper	HarperCollins Publishers, Inc.
Harvard UP	Harvard University Press
Heath	D. C. Heath
HMSO	Her (or His) Majesty's Stationery Office (British)

Houghton	Houghton Mifflin Co.
Knopf	Alfred A. Knopf, Inc.
Little	Little, Brown and Company, Inc.
Louisiana State UP	Louisiana State University Press
Macmillan	Macmillan Publishing Company, Inc.
McGraw	McGraw-Hill, Inc.
MLA	The Modern Language Association of America
NCTE	The National Council of Teachers of English
NEA	The National Education Association
Norton	W. W. Norton and Co., Inc.
Oxford UP	Oxford University Press
Prentice	Prentice Hall, Inc.
Random	Random House, Inc.
Scribner's	Charles Scribner's Sons
Simon	Simon and Schuster, Inc.
SIRS	Social Issues Resources Series
St. Martin's	St. Martin's Press, Inc.
UMI	University Microfilms International
U of Chicago P	University of Chicago Press
U of South Carolina P	University of South Carolina Press
U of Texas P	University of Texas Press
Yale UP	Yale University Press

Colacurcio, Michael J. "Footsteps of Ann Hutchinson: The Context of <u>The Scarlet Letter</u>." <u>ELH</u> 39 (1972): 459–94. Rpt. in part in Gross et al. 213–30.

Crane, Stephen. "The Open Boat." McMichael 1535–52.

Crews, Frederick C. "The Ruined Wall." <u>The Sins of the Fathers: Hawthorne's Psychological Themes</u>. New York: Oxford UP, 1966. 136–53. Rpt. in Gross et al. 361–71.

Fogle, Richard Harter. "[Realms of Being and Dramatic Irony.]" <u>Hawthorne's Fiction: The Light and the Dark</u>. Norman: U of Oklahoma P, 1952. 106–18. Rpt. in Gross et al. 308–15.

Frost, Robert. "Mending Wall." Kennedy and Gioia 1065–66.

---. "The Road Not Taken." Kennedy and Gioia 910–11.

Gibaldi, Joseph. <u>MLA Handbook for Writers of Research Papers</u>. 5th ed. New York: Mod. Lang. Assn., 1999.

---. <u>MLA Style Manual and Guide to Scholarly Publishing</u>. 2nd ed. New York: Mod. Lang. Assn., 1998.

Gross, Seymour, et al., eds. <u>The Scarlet Letter: An Authoritative Text, Essays in Criticism and Scholarship</u>. 3rd ed. Norton Critical Edition. New York: Norton, 1988.

Harnack, Andrew, and Eugene Kleppinger. <u>Online: A Reference Guide to Using Internet Sources</u>. Boston: Bedford-St. Martin's, 2000.

Hawthorne, Nathaniel. "Young Goodman Brown." <u>Uncommon Knowledge: Exploring Ideas through Reading and Writing</u>. Ed. Rose Hawkins and Robert Isaacson. Boston: Houghton, 1996. 336–47.

---. <u>The Scarlet Letter</u>. Gross et al. 1–178.

Herbert, George. "Easter Wings." Kennedy and Gioia 892.

Kennedy, X. J., and Dana Gioia, eds. <u>Literature: An Introduction to Fiction, Poetry, and Drama</u>. 7th ed. New York: Longman-Addison, 1999.

McMichael, George, ed. <u>Concise Anthology of American Literature</u>. 4th ed. Upper Saddle River, NJ: Prentice, 1998.

McNamara, Anne Marie. "The Character of Flame: The Function of Pearl in <u>The Scarlet Letter</u>." <u>American Literature</u> 27 (1956): 537–53.

Miller, Arthur. <u>Death of a Salesman</u>. Kennedy and Gioia 1636–1707.

<u>MLA Style: Documenting Sources from the World Wide Web</u>. 8 Dec. 1999. Modern Language Association of America. 30 Jan. 2000 <http://www.mla.org/style/sources.htm>.

Stubbs, John Caldwell. "<u>The Scarlet Letter</u>: 'A Tale of Human Frailty and Sorrow.'" <u>The Pursuit of Form: A Study of Hawthorne and the Romance</u>. Urbana: U of Illinois P, 1970. 81–102. Rpt. in Gross et al. 384–92.

Trimmer, Joseph F. <u>A Guide to MLA Documentation</u>. 5th ed. Boston: Houghton, 1999.

Twain, Mark [Samuel Langhorne Clemens]. <u>The Adventures of Huckleberry Finn</u>. McMichael 1235–1419.

Whitman, Walt. "The Wound-Dresser." <u>Complete Poetry and Selected Prose</u>. Ed. James E. Miller, Jr. Riverside Edition. Boston: Houghton, 1959. 220–22.